Bill Giovannetti has given the church a fantastic treasure! On most every page I found myself vacillating between a heart-humbling gratitude for God's total embrace and a heart-pounding desire to stand up and cheer! This book boldly teaches us how a ch con-fidence of the Father's full approval i illed with heavy-handed demands and prc you will return to again and again to help eely in the rich atmosphere of amazing g sely practical, and deeply liberating! Don't miss out!

—Jeremy White, pastor and author of
The Gospel Uncut: Learning to Rest in the Grace of God

Today's evangelical leaders, in their zeal to move beyond aisle-walking, hand-raising, "cheap grace" Christianity, are pushing believers toward a more radical, activist faith. But is busyness the mark of a true believer? Or is it just a "cooler, hipper" form of legalism? With humor and clarity, Pastor Bill Giovannetti lovingly offers a sound prescription for producing true Christ-embracing, Spirit-empowered, God-exalting disciples: a full-body dive into the ocean of God's riches—at Christ's expense.

—Linda J. White, award-winning author of three
FBI thrillers, including *Seeds of Evidence*

With this book, the author, also a pastor and professor, meets a deep, gen-uine need in today's church and brightens the spirit of every reader with his eye-opening intervention of Grace.

—Mary Tatem, author of story-based devotional books including
The Quilt of Life, The Quilt of Faith, and *The Quilt of Joy*

Like dawn's first burst of daylight, *Grace Intervention* illuminates the truth that grace is the unmerited work of God in our lives—regardless of what we've earned, worked for, or deserved. This book sets free those who strug-gle to wiggle out from beneath the weight of expectations imposed by legalists. With wisdom and genuineness, Bill Giovannetti exposes the new face of legalism and offers solid teaching that encourages us to tune our hearts to grace and live freely in God's glory.

—Megan DiMaria, author, speaker, a prisoner of hope

In this insightful and daring analysis of the modern church, Bill Giovannetti sees through the hash-tagging, hipster appeal of neo-legalism and identifies the symptoms of Christianity's worst disease: Grace Deficit Disorder. *Grace Intervention* is a breath of fresh air for Christians who are tired of playing games and doing their duty. It is an emphatic declaration of God's good and gracious commitment to you!

—Paul Ellis, bestselling author of
The Big House and *The Gospel in Twenty Questions*

Prepare yourself. Every pre-conception you have concerning grace is about to be challenged to the core. Pastor Bill Giovannetti's *Grace Intervention* is a much-needed game changer for the way we do church.

—Michael K. Reynolds, author of the award-winning
Heirs of Ireland series

Whether you agree with Pastor Bill Giovannetti's conclusions or not, this theology of grace addresses the major tenets of grace and is a must read for believers from all theological camps. . . . Take your time reading and reflecting on these fifteen chapters—they may just change your life addressing that "Grace Deficit Disorder" that so many of us have experienced!

—Rev. Patrick A. Blewett, D.Min., Ph.D. Dean,
A.W. Tozer Theological Seminary

So often the "shoulds" and "should nots" in life threaten to overwhelm my joy, and I get lost in a sea of guilt and hopelessness. But God never intended that for us, and Bill Giovannetti's beautiful look at grace empowered me to look to Him—instead of to a hopeless world—for the grace I so desperately need. Every person who has ever felt burdened by a legalistic Christian world, by hopelessness or guilt, or even by the pain of feeling unforgiven, will find hope and healing in *Grace Intervention*.

—Erin MacPherson, author of The Christian Mama's Guide series

This is a refreshing, well written, and engaging book which challenges believers to "come to fully understand the significance of God's staggeringly beautiful grace and rest secure, knowing that your life with Him starts with grace, ends with grace, and rests on grace in between."

—Stephen R. Lewis, Th.M., Ph.D.
President
Rocky Mountain Bible College
Rocky Mountain Seminary

Grace is a term we use loosely but often misunderstand. With his much-needed book, *Grace Intervention*, Bill Giovannetti offers a beautiful narrative of grace to help Christians break the chains of legalism that subconsciously bind so many of us.

—Allison K. Flexer, author of *Truth, Lies, and the Single Woman*

Me, a legalist? What I thought about grace was awakened and deepened through *Grace Intervention*. Giovannetti's book is written with depth, humor, honesty and, well, a whole lot of grace. At times, it's a hard look in the mirror. A must read for every person seeking an authentic and grace-filled life with Christ.

—Cindy (Martinusen) Coloma, bestselling author of *Winter Passing*, *The Orchid House* and *The Salt Garden*

UNDERSTANDING
GOD'S BEAUTIFUL
GIFT OF GRACE

INTERVENTION

grace

BILL
GIOVANNETTI

SHILOH RUN  PRESS
An Imprint of Barbour Publishing, Inc.

Published by Shiloh Run Press, an imprint of Barbour Publishing, Inc., P.O. Box 719, Uhrichsville, Ohio 44683, www.shilohrunpress.com.

Our mission is to publish and distribute inspirational products offering exceptional value and biblical encouragement to the masses.

Member of the
Evangelical Christian
Publishers Association

Printed in the United States of America.

DEDICATION

*This book is for everybody who struggles
to accept God's acceptance of them.*

ACKNOWLEDGMENTS

I've been on the receiving end of other people's grace all my life: from my parents, my family, the churches that reared me, and every preacher, author, and teacher who's ever shined a light on Jesus and his love. Thank you. I'm grateful to Art Rorheim and the late Lance B. Latham, founders of Awana, for standing firm for grace.

Thank you, Kelly McIntosh, and the whole team at Barbour Publishing, for believing in this project. I'm ever grateful to the brightest star in the literary constellation, my agent, Janet Kobobel Grant, and to the family of "Bookies" whose wisdom guides me every day. Denise Giovannetti contributed invaluable assistance as an early reader, and Joe Giovannetti helped clarify and strengthen key parts of this book; you are loved and appreciated.

There's a huge thank you in my heart for the people and leaders of Neighborhood Church. It's a privilege to be your pastor and to experience grace with you.

I could not write a syllable without the support and love of my precious wife, Margi. You are brilliant, wise, fun, beautiful, and true. Thank you for making me a better man. My awesome kids, Josie and J.D., show me every day what grace looks like. I love you more than you can know.

Above all, thanks be to God for His unspeakable gift. Where would I be without Christ's great love?

CONTENTS

INTERVENTION

My friend Jason and his college buddies had splurged on a nice hotel for spring break. One afternoon, he and the guys decided to hang out at the hotel swimming pool. At the far end of the patio, a few girls were sunning themselves. Jason decided to swim over and flirt.

He flexed his pecs, dived into the pool, and swam over to where the girls were sitting. Quickly striking up a conversation, he soon had all the girls laughing. He glanced back at his buddies, who pretended not to be jealous.

Jason focused on the cutest girl. Soon he was sitting on the edge of the pool, talking just with her. She smiled and giggled and laughed, and Jason felt studly and strong. Offering to grab some sodas, he bounded over to the vending machine. That's when he made his awful discovery.

As he approached the shaded area where the vending machines stood, he passed a window and stole a quick, self-admiring glance at his reflection. Something caught his eye. Something wrong. Something on his face.

Suddenly, he understood why the girls had been laughing so much. Why their smiles were so big. They weren't laughing *with* him; they were laughing *at* him. For there, plastered on his face, running from nose to ear, was a thick, green rope of snot.

With his face now burning red, he dropped off the soda to the girl, mumbled an excuse, and slinked back to his friends.

Sometimes you can have a problem and you're the last to know.

The Invisible Problem

What if Christianity has a problem that we can't see? One that's tough to detect without seeing a reflection of ourselves? What if there's a big snot rope running across our faces and everybody's laughing at us, but we don't get it?

Sometimes, the most loving thing a person can do is grab your attention and in the plainest of words say, "Hey, you've got snot on your face."

In the church, legalism is the biggest, most destructive, and toughest to detect string of snot ever sneezed by Satan over the people of God.

Most Christians, myself included, have that snot on our faces.

Legalism infects entire swaths of Christianity. It worms its way into relationships. It sneaks into books and conferences. It is shouted from pulpits. And it buries itself in the deepest recesses of the human heart, stealing a treasure not rightly its own.

It can look so good, but it feels so bad. It preaches well, yet it can make its hearers "twice as much a son of hell" (Matthew

23:15) as they were when they started.

It launches followers around the world to do the work of Christ, but with empty gas tanks, doomed to fizzle out or fake it until they just give up.

✓ Legalism vacuums the joy out of a room. It quenches the spirit. It is a vampire in Christian clothing, sucking out the faintest spark of divine life.

As fast as God weaves a garment of grace, legalism unravels it. As fast as a new convert can say, "Please save me," legalists rush in to get a signature on salvation's fine print.

All the church's super-leaders, with their calls to world-changing radicalism, with their crazy-high-demand love for God, with their summons to be more spiritual than Jesus—don't they realize most of us are already pedaling as fast as we can? Don't they see how they're flogging us into depression and shame?

Why should an already frazzled world come to our churches when they know all we'll do is pile more duties onto their already backed-up do-to lists? "We're barely making it," people say. "We're hardly getting by. We can't keep up with you freaks."

They look at busy Christians and see fakes. They see ultra-spirituality fronting bedraggled souls—frayed, worn out, dysfunctional, and shallow—slapping on a happy face to change the world for Jesus.

✓ Hey legalists: stop talking at us.

✓ First fix the mess inside your own four walls; then maybe give us a call.

Making the Church Safe for Normal Christians

I am writing with a great love for the church and with great compassion for its people. I believe the church, resting in the grace of God, is the hope of the world. I want to join the chorus of voices already calling legalism out of hiding. I want to shove it into a sea of forgetfulness.

And I want to make the church safe for normal Christians.

Safe for seekers and doubters, addicts, and therapists.

Safe for humble people.

Safe for broken people with more problems than solutions.

A humble mom struggling through her kid's math homework performs a noble deed, as much the work of God as Billy Graham standing in the pulpit before tens of thousands.

A single dad, pushing a strand of hair from his forehead with one hand as he struggles to change a diaper with the other, is doing something radical for Jesus.

So is a student hitting the books, a truck driver delivering goods, and a grandma slouched in her wheelchair praying. They may never make it to Africa. They may never suffer persecution—thank God. No one will ever ask for an autograph or cheer their names.

But God is pleased.

If the message we proclaim doesn't work for a blue-collar guy who changes oil to put bread on his family's table—if the kind of radicalism we demand makes his life of no account— then we have not understood the grace of Jesus.

If the message we embrace makes heroes out of the church's activists and a second-class disciple of the janitor pushing the broom, then we have not understood the grace of Jesus. We've been slimed by legalism.

✔ If the message we believe puts parenting on a lower plane than prayer, puts resting (Mary) on a lower plane than serving (Martha), or puts burger flipping on a lower plane than preaching, then we have not understood the grace of Jesus. We've exalted legalism to the place of honor and evaporated grace into a misty haze.

Either Christianity works for the frazzled and frumpy struggling to just get by, or it doesn't work at all.

Enough with the ultra-spiritual demands.

Enough with the legalism.

It's okay to pray for "a quiet and peaceable life" (1 Timothy 2:2).

Jesus is good with a cup of cold water.

The only "should" here is to rest your weary self in the matchless grace of God.

That's radical. God delights in that.

Rest in the promise that he will complete the work he started the day he scooped you into his loving embrace. That's radical, too.

So pour some stale coffee in that Styrofoam cup. Dump in a packet of sugar and some powdered creamer, and plant yourself on that metal folding chair.

It's time for your grace intervention.

Oh, and you might want to wipe that snot off your face.

By the way, my name is Bill. And I'm a recovering legalist.

CHAPTER 1

TERMS

If it were the throne of justice—we might fear; or if it were the throne of holiness—we might be dazzled with its splendors. But it is the throne of grace—where God meets sinners on the principles of grace; where God confers on seeking souls grace to help them in time of need; and where he manifests the deepest, tenderest sympathy for miserable and wretched men.
JAMES SMITH (1800S)

Yesterday's legalists were obvious. They shunned dancing, movies, drinking, and rock music. Their daughters wore ankle-length skorts. The men sported crew cuts, toted massive black Bibles, and cast haughty glances at any pitiful reprobate who didn't wear a suit to church. Yesterday's legalists stood out like Baptists in a mosh pit.

Today's legalists run the mosh pit.

They've evolved a cooler, hipper legalism—complete with microbrews, body piercings, and wine-bar worship. But it's every bit as malignant as the legalism of their rhythmically challenged grandparents.

The snake has shed its skin, but it's still the same old snake: humans, by human effort, seeking the approval of God.

We humans are legalists to the core, twisting the grand story of God's work for us into the fairy tale of our works for him. We easily morph grace into religiosity and the gospel into human achievement. Legalism has been the church's death-of-a-thousand-cuts for two thousand years.

And it didn't go away when Christ's followers started dancing. We just think it did. After all, what clear-minded observer would tag a drinking, dancing, pierced, tattooed, rabbi-bearded, Vans-shod, smart phone-sporting Jesus person as a legalist? Antinomian, maybe. Licentious, possibly. But legalist? Never.

Not, at least, until we define our terms. Once we understand what legalism really is, today's legalists stand out like bird droppings on a windshield.

We need an intervention. We need a loving confrontation to throw a wrench in our soul's self-defeating legalistic machinery.

Here it is.

I write as a lover of *legalists* and hater of *legalism*. I don't have much choice but to love legalists, because I've been a perpetrator for years. Had I been born in an earlier era, I might have been an Inquisitor. As a longtime pastor, I've had ample opportunity to demonstrate my religious superiority. I can even sling around Greek and Hebrew words to make my case.

Part of recovery is admitting where you're coming from.

I've also been loved and nurtured by people who truly loved God, but whose faith was infected with legalism. They shunned movies, dancing, drinking, playing cards, and long-haired males, even as they loved and blessed me better than I deserved.

The legalism bug hopped from person to person in our cloistered fellowship. When one minister with a nationwide following was criticized because his hair touched his ears, and a woman was criticized for wearing a pantsuit to church, I suspected something was up. When an older mentor told me to quit teaching kids that they couldn't lose salvation— because I was giving license to sin—I was convinced.

★ It's hard for me to criticize the self-giving, good-hearted church families who reared me. I love them, and they loved me. I just can't stand the legalism embedded in their message and driven into my psyche.

So, I'd like to clarify what that legalistic message is and isn't, and how it might rear its head in today's pseudo-liberated churches.

Legalism: [n. lee'-gul-ism] doing good stuff for God while bypassing the power of God.

God has always called the church to do good works in the world. But he calls us to do those works in *his* power, not our own. And he calls us to do those works as *an expression* of Christ's life within us.

Take away the mystery of Christ in us and what good are we? What makes us stand out from the Peace Corps, the Red Cross, or the Red Crescent, for that matter? In our rush to "give back," "pay it forward," "make a difference," and "change our world," have we devolved into a churchified version of *Oprah*? Humanitarianism with a little Jesus sprinkled on top?

Could it be we're offering the world a Pharisee-scented church without even noticing?

The Bible brands our good works—no matter how well-intentioned or on point—as dead works, when they are done in the power of the flesh (Hebrews 6:1, 9:14). When answering the question, "Who can be saved?" Jesus said, "With man this is impossible" (Mark 10:27 NIV).

Humans doing the work of God by human effort—in search of the divine "attaboy"—is still the nucleus of legalism's virus.

A past generation denounced this as "works righteousness."

Here's the grand premise of all theology: *only God can please God.*

I can't. You can't. Bono can't. In and of ourselves, we are the walking dead. As the late Ray Stedman said, "The most widespread form of legality [legalism] in the Christian church is the flesh—trying to do something before God which will be acceptable to him."[1]

Absent an infiltration of God's own virtue, even the finest work of human hands sizzles into nothingness under the heat of the divine gaze. God will not dwell in a house made by human hands, he says, yet Christians haphazardly hammer two-by-fours together and call it good.

It isn't good. Nothing is good without a touch from God, because only he can achieve that which pleases himself. You can't do good stuff for God—and have it count—while bypassing his power. Only God can please God.

Let's start with that premise and see where it leads.

Traditional legalism: the rule-oriented legalism that spawned worship wars, skorts, and evangelicals who can't dance.

I'm old enough to have witnessed the birth of Christian rock. The Christian bookstore in downtown Chicago, where I lived, wouldn't sell it. No Amy Grant. No Petra. No Chuck Girard. No groovy rhythms or drum-driven beats.

The main Christian radio station in town refused to play it. Churches split over it.

Then they "blended" it with traditional music, which made everybody miserable, like simmering a stew with at least one vegetable every diner hates.

Worship wars are a hazy memory in most circles, but could the spirit that animated them still be alive and well in today's hipper, wiser churches?

What comes to mind when you hear the word *legalism?* All the religious rules and taboos of past generations? Me, too. That's what I mean by *traditional legalism.*

This variety—my own particular lifeblood—thrived on extra-biblical rules, self-righteous sanctimony, and the unwitting baptism of cultural values. Traditional legalists admired each other's social backwardness. Just stay one generation behind the times in music, dress, and language, and you're okay.

Traditional legalists specialized in moralistic codes against drinking, dancing, movies, theater, card playing, pants on women, makeup, smoking, and rock and roll. They added their own laws to God's. They reduced a life-giving relationship with the heavenly Father to a predictable sequence of religious steps. They congratulated each other's superficial conformity to the club's unspoken rules, while in many cases their hearts were far from God.

They had the form of godliness, but they denied its power. I'll use the term *traditional legalism* to specify the easily caricatured legalism of yesteryear.

Contrast this with *neo-legalism.*

Neo-legalism: [adj. nee-oh, "new"] the stealthy legalism of today's up-to-date churches.

Where traditional legalists offer their personal holiness to God, neo-legalists offer social benevolence. Where traditional legalists offer doctrinal correctness, neo-legalists offer relational tolerance. Where traditional legalists offer rigid adherence to biblical words, neo-legalists offer free-flowing responsiveness to an ever-speaking voice, presumably God's.

All are good things, perhaps.

But all are equally legalistic when fueled by the flesh—the rancid power of human nature devoid of the power of God. Remember, only God can please God; and unless he is working through you, nothing you do makes the cut. Just because you do good things doesn't make them God things.

When you work for God, strive for God, worship God, or wave your hands in the air for God by any power but God's, you've picked up the parasite of legalism.

In their rush to reverse their grandparents' legalism, neo-legalists created a legalism of their own—an inverse legalism that leaves the church just as graceless as before.

Jesus warned the scribes and Pharisees, "Even so you also

outwardly appear righteous to men, but inside you are full of hypocrisy and lawlessness" (Matthew 23:28).

Think about this:

Lawfulness on the outside. Impressive to religious people.

Lawlessness on the inside. Not impressive to God.

Apparently, human skin comprises the thin line between legalism and lawlessness (antinomianism, to be technical). Neo-legalists rush to change the world but have scarcely paused to change their own hearts.

This is what makes neo-legalism so stealthy. The outside seems so good: we love life's losers; we embrace sinners; we love prodigals. We accept everybody. Just as they are. And it's okay that they stay just as they are.

Surely, this spirit incarnates the perfect combination of grace and truth that Jesus exemplified. Right?

"How could anyone call us legalists?" the neo-legalist wonders. "We're not shunning anyone. We're not laying arbitrary rules on anyone's back. Hell, we even cuss once in a while! And we had an open bar at our church Christmas experience, and our pastor disciples us poolside amid the sweet incense of premium cigars. How can you call us legalists?"

Simple. You have mashed the vast quality called grace into the thimble of indiscriminate leniency and have forgotten the power of God.

Grace: the unmerited favor of a non-lenient God.

My wife teaches business law at a Christian university. After a particularly gruesome exam, Margi asked the class why they had crashed and burned. The students had no good excuse.

Most confessed to a lack of study. One plucky student seized the chance to grovel. He said, "Your husband talks about grace all the time; why don't you show us grace?" Others chimed in. The flunkards begged for grades better than they deserved.

No deal.

They whined. *Why no grace?*

This led to a convicting conversation about real grace, especially its polar distinction from leniency.

Grace satisfies justice and empowers the one who embraces it.

Leniency bypasses justice and debilitates the one who embraces it.

God is "just and the justifier of the one who has faith in Jesus" (Romans 3:26). He does not—he cannot—skip straight to the good stuff without first body slamming sin to the mat and adjusting the maladjusted sinner to his immutable character. This he did at the hill called Calvary, where Christ poured out his lifeblood as a ransom. No sane person contemplating the Cross can conclude that grace equals leniency.

God isn't lenient. He can't be. He can't sacrifice his holiness on the altar of love; he would cease being God.

Love can't win unless holiness wins, too.

But neo-legalists imply this all the time. Some even write books about it. A generation suckled by a one-dimensional God of love has transmogrified him from a righteous heavenly Father into an unassertive heavenly Grandfather. More like a fairy godmother, less like Gandalf.

What is grace?

It's hard to define because it is so comprehensive. In grace,

God adapts his provision to suit the vast panorama of human need. Grace, therefore, is a situational shape-shifter.

Grace is God doing for you what you can't do for yourself. It is everything God is free to do for you on the basis of the Cross.

Grace is your not earning, not deserving, not meriting, not winning, not working.

Grace is God empowering, the Spirit indwelling, and Christ living through you day by day.

Grace is the supernatural power to live each moment of every day to the fullest, for the glory of God, and the ultimate satisfaction of your own soul.

Grace is turning from self to God, from self-effort to Christ effort, from working to resting and trusting in a God who will see you through.

If you need it, grace supplies it.

If you break it, grace fixes it.

If you lose it, grace finds it.

If you spoil it, grace restores it.

If you regret it, grace forgives it.

If you're sick, grace heals.

If you're dirty, grace cleanses.

If you're down low, grace lifts you up.

If you're up high, grace brings you down.

Where you hurt, grace comforts.

Where you fear, grace fortifies.

Where you doubt, grace convinces.

Where you can't, grace can.

For the deluded, grace brings truth.

For the addicted, grace brings freedom.

For the dysfunctional, grace brings wholeness.

For the lonely, grace brings love.

For the lost, grace brings a salvation so far reaching that words can't do it justice.

Grace is the work of God, doing the thing you need, exactly when you need it done, on the basis of the finished work of Christ, not on the basis of what you've earned or deserved.

What is grace? Grace is God's fierce, kind, joyful, gentle, rough, gruff, never-failing fathering of his adopted children through all life's crazy twists and turns, always with an eye toward the Cross and the blessings Christ secured.

The worst thing that can ever happen to you as a child of God is to forget your blood-bought grace.

This forgetfulness, unfortunately, has risen to epidemic proportions in the church today. That's why I'm writing about it. We're going to give this forgetfulness a name: Grace Deficit Disorder (GDD).

> **Grace Deficit Disorder (GDD):** the mental, emotional, and spiritual problems— and countless manifestations—resulting from a person's failure to fully appropriate grace.

Grace Deficit Disorder manifests as ignorance of grace, misunderstanding of grace, failure to utilize grace, doubtfulness of grace, repudiation of grace, contradiction of grace, or any mental construct in which grace is grounded in any effort other than the finished work of the Cross.

Grace Deficit Disorder always triggers legalism.

Life is needlessly hard for Christians who suffer from

GDD. God hands down a daily supply of grace, but they don't see it. Or they don't know how to use it. Or they see it and know how to use it but prefer to go on in their own strength.

So they crash. They burn out. They fail.

They flunk the business law exam.

Grace is not simply a policy of God's; it is also the *power* of God installed into his children, enabling them to do good stuff, such as studying for exams and stamping out poverty. My wife didn't neglect grace by giving her students the mediocre grades they had earned; her students neglected grace when they chilled at the coffee shop rather than using God's power to crack open the books and study.

> **Gracification:** [n. gray'-sif-i-kay'-shun, also adj. gracified] the process by which God flips our spiritual, doctrinal, and emotional arrows so that they finally point in the right direction.

Let's foment a revolution in today's church. It's time to unleash the awesome power of gracification. Only gracification can cure Grace Deficit Disorder. There's never been another remedy.

First, a little exam. C'mon, no whining.

In the next fifteen seconds, contemplate the word commitment in light of your life with God. Think of three or four mental bullet points about commitment—whatever comes to mind. In a Christian context, what does *commitment* mean?

Ready? Go!

ONE-one thousand, TWO-one thousand...FIFTEEN-one thousand.

Time!

What did you come up with? When I give that little exam in conversations and talks, here are the usual bullet points that come up:

- Dedication
- Serving God
- Enduring tough times
- Being faithful to God
- Showing good character
- Staying true no matter what
- Standard "I am committed to God" stuff

Odds are strong your list was in that ballpark.

So here's my big question: *Is Christianity's core message more about* your *commitment to God or about* his *commitment to you?* Why doesn't God's commitment ever make the list?

In English class, I learned about two kinds of sentences that are relevant here: declarative and imperative. Declarative sentences declare facts and make statements; they inform us. Imperative sentences issue commands; they obligate us.

The great bulk of the Bible is declarative, not imperative. God has told us what is, what was, and what will be. He has declared his boundless charity for messed-up mankind. He has revealed his complete forgiveness as the starting point—not the ending point—of all our efforts to be holy. He has lit up the story of Jesus and his incomparable sacrifice as a spectacle to dazzle humans and angels for eternity. And with unbreakable chains, he has linked every benefit he sends our way to history's climactic moment at the Cross and Resurrection of Christ.

God has darkened the theater of the cosmos and aimed his dazzling spotlight on Jesus Christ—on his self-giving, self-sacrificing love. God has made his own commitment to us the centerpiece of the cosmic story, rendering you and me and everybody else as bit players in the drama of redemption.

The Bible declares God's nature, attributes, relationships, gifts, blessings, mercy, kindness, goodness, benevolence, self-sufficiency, self-sacrifice, riches, generosity, plan, and central promise (and all subsidiary promises radiating from it).

The Bible tells the tale of God's grace unfolding in the real lives of morally bedraggled people.

It is the self-revelation of a God who is infinitely more committed to us than we will ever be to him.

It is *declarative* above all else.

Why then, do our sermons, songs, and books emphasize the imperative? Why do we spend so much time telling people what to do (or *not* do) before we have fueled their spirits with what God has already done?

Our proportions are out of whack. Commit! Submit! Give! Serve! Go! Sacrifice! Be radical for Jesus! Give back! Change the world! Be nice! Be a good husband/wife/mom/dad/single/employer/employee/friend/church person/greenie/global citizen/scout! These, and a thousand other imperatives, rise off the church like the wavy lines of cartoon stink from a road-killed skunk.

Meanwhile, we get the declarative stuff wrong (what little we even transmit): a contorted message of insipid love from an impossibly dull God.

Arrows

Let's talk about arrows, shall we?

When we consider the part of the story where we do stuff for God, let's imagine an arrow pointing up, from us to God. The arrow indicates the direction of the benefit—in this case, from us to God.

When we consider the part of the story where God does stuff for us, we'll point the arrow down, from God to us.

Arrows pointing up represent works (everything we do for God).

Arrows pointing down represent grace (everything God does for us).

Gracification happens when God flips the arrows in our souls, to correct their direction and proportion. He makes the biggest, fattest, juiciest arrows of grace point downward from himself to us. He makes the skinny, minority, arrows of duty point upward from us to him.

It's biblical: "We love Him because He first loved us" (1 John 4:19).

Translation: until the fattest, biggest, most-est arrows in your imagination point from God to you, it will be impossible for you to love God the way he wants you to love him.

I need gracification. You need gracification. All God's children need gracification.

You know you're gracified when the word *commitment* conjures thick, juicy arrows pointing down from God to you—when what leaps to the front of your imagination is the incomparable commitment that Jesus displayed on Calvary's cross.

By nature, legalism owns our instincts; we're born that way. We're fallen members of a fallen race, hopelessly addicted to religious self-effort.

We need to displace our native legalism with grace. Grace must become our knee-jerk reaction: a grace rooted in God's forgiveness, God's generosity, God's kindness, and God's love. Not because we're temperamentally weak, but because we've got the love of Jesus deep in our hearts, and we've been gracified.

Want some extra fun? The next time you go to church, draw arrows. First draw a cloud at the top of a blank page, and write *God* inside it. Next, draw a stick figure of yourself at the bottom of the page, and label it *Me*. Now, for every worship element, song, sermon, or video, draw an arrow. When the worship element emphasizes your commitment to God, draw an upward arrow from you to God. When it emphasizes God's commitment to you, draw a downward arrow down from God to you. Draw your arrows fat or skinny to indicate intensity or energy or how much the preacher shouted.

Do this for a month of Sundays. (You can do this in the margins of Christian books, too.)

Don't go waving your arrow charts in your church leaders' faces, insisting they swallow the gracification pill. That would make you (a) a jerk, (b) a nut, and (c) ungracious.

Just see if you notice what I think you'll notice: your arrows are out of whack. They're disproportionate and pointing the wrong way. We need gracification, *stat!*

An old, dead preacher once said, "For every look at self, take ten looks at Christ."

That's what I'm talking about.

CHAPTER 2

OVERLOAD

I have heard it put like this: There was a boatman and two theologians in a boat, and one was arguing that salvation was by faith and the other by works. The boatman listened, and then said, "Let me tell you how it looks to me. Suppose I call this oar Faith and this one Works. If I pull on this one, the boat goes around; if I pull on this other one, it goes around the other way, but if I pull on both oars, I get you across the river." I have heard many preachers use that illustration to prove that we are saved by faith and works. That might do if we were going to heaven in a rowboat, but we are not. We are carried on the shoulders of the Shepherd, who came seeking lost sheep. When He finds them, He carries them home on His shoulders.[2]

DR. HARRY IRONSIDE

Cliché Melee

When I first found the above quote from Harry Ironside, a former pastor of Chicago's historic Moody Church, I posted it on Facebook. A lot of my friends immediately "liked" it. Maybe that's because they've been gracified.

Other friends didn't get it. They thought Ironside—and I, by posting it—endorsed the oar story, the fallacy that salvation requires faith plus works. For the record, it doesn't.

One Facebook friend commented, "The subscription to salvation is free, but the annual renewal costs you everything."

I hate Christian clichés.

Here's a popular one: "If he isn't Lord of all, he isn't Lord at all."

Christ is Lord, no doubt. But my childhood preachers pushed me over the edge with this one. The first time I heard it, my inner bookkeeper performed a quick moral inventory and decided that Jesus wasn't Lord of all. Lord of some, definitely. Lord of most, maybe. But Lord of all, not even close. Since he wasn't Lord of all, he wasn't Lord at all. Therefore, I was doomed.

That pretty much sums up almost two decades of spiritual upbringing for a sincere Italian boy growing up in Chicago. I felt like that kid in fifth grade who acted up once or twice and was marked forever as a troublemaker. Teacher had her eye on him.

And God had his eye on me. He wasn't Lord of all, so I'd better get cracking.

Other clichés piled on. Surrender all. Yield. Commit. Give your life to Christ. Give him your all.

I was gasping for air, pedaling as fast as I could.

The youth pastor in a high school group I attended preached that the way to heaven was to "follow Jesus." He said it meant doing what Jesus would do. I was confused, so after the meeting, I grilled him. "When did you first receive Jesus?" I asked. He said it was maybe five or six years ago. Then I asked, "Have you consistently 'followed Jesus' for those five or six years?"

He got mad and walked away.

Is the way to God a function of what I do for him or of what he has done for me? Is it possible most Christian clichés are just nasty little symptoms of GDD?

Before the *Left Behind* books and movies, there was the legendary 1970s end-time film *A Thief in the Night*. That film scared me straight about a dozen times. Don't get me wrong; I'm sure God used it in amazing ways. It's just that when you watch it today, it's remarkably un-hip. In one scene, Jenny—a pig-tailed teenager—returns to Teen Town to learn more about salvation. Here's how that snappy dialogue goes:

> Teen Town Counselor: *That's right, Jenny. In a way, it is free. What I mean is, it doesn't cost anything but your life.*
>
> Jenny: *That sounds pretty expensive.*
>
> Teen Town Counselor: *Well, it might seem that way, until you realize that you're letting the God who created you, the God who cares for you more than any other person could. . .that you're letting him take over.*[3]

Let me get this straight: "It doesn't cost anything but your life," yet it's free.

You're letting God "take over," yet it's free.

My teenage brain was exploding. In what universe do these

mismatches match? Only in the bizarro world of Christian clichés.

The Trouble with Cliches

If salvation is a mansion, something called the gospel is its threshold. No one crawls in through a window or climbs down the chimney. The only way in is through a subset of all biblical doctrine, called the gospel. No wonder the world's best church planter delivered a firm whack upside the head to any would-be gospel tinkerers: "But even if we, or an angel from heaven, preach any other gospel to you than what we have preached to you, let him be accursed" (Galatians 1:8).

When I was nine, my parents forced me into piano lessons. I'd rather have been playing baseball, but there I sat, on Mrs. Zissis's piano bench, torturing Handel, Haydn, and Thompson. My teacher insisted I play each piece perfectly before moving on to the next. I struggled with Bach's Prelude in G for a couple of weeks, until, one golden afternoon, I got it right. As the final notes faded into musical history, I tacked on my own embellishment (a simple low D followed by a low G—*ta-da!*). I sent a look of smug satisfaction Mrs. Zissis's way.

I'll never forget the mortified look on her face. Her eyes grew wide. Her jaw dropped. She gasped. She rose to her full five-foot stature and said, "Bill Giovannetti does not improve on Johann Sebastian Bach!"

Nobody improves on the gospel of Jesus Christ. To alter it is to mar it.

It's at precisely this point that we stumble over our hornet's nest of Christian clichés. They embellish the gospel. They invariably deconstruct the good news of grace into the bad news of high-demand human performance.

Case in point: "Give your life to Christ." Really? Exactly who is the giver and who is the receiver in the equation of salvation? And exactly what life do we have that we can give to God? Aren't we dead in our trespasses? (See Ephesians 2:1 and Colossians 2:13 for what Paul says about that.)

I struggled as a teenager because I couldn't figure out which way the arrows pointed. Legalism owned me.

The Gospel of Grace

If the gospel is anything, it is the story of a gargantuan arrow pointing down from God to us. "Christ died for our sins, according to the Scriptures," Paul summarizes. "He was buried [and] rose again the third day according to the Scriptures" (1 Corinthians 15:3–4). This is what Paul calls the gospel. It is the whole gospel. God gave. We receive.

"Christ died." That is *history*—heaven and earth's darkest moment.

"Christ died for our sins." That is *theology*—the theology of substitutionary atonement.

The church's task is to keep telling that bit of history, coupled with that bit of theology, over and over in words and actions that every generation understands, thereby summoning men and women everywhere to embrace the Savior, Jesus. We'll dig down into what this means in chapter 10.

I won't quibble over your particular formulation of the gospel, but I will fight like a junkyard dog that the Cross of Christ gets its due prominence.

He died; we live. He gave; we receive. He sacrificed; we say thank you. He paid the price; we grow rich. He gave his life *for* us, that he might give his life *to* us, and live his life *through* us. Any other gospel inverts the arrows. Any other gospel is not good news. Any other gospel invites God's curse on the preacher.

Paul's entire life demonstrated a laser-beam focus "to testify to the gospel of the grace of God" (Acts 20:24). John announced, "For the law was given through Moses, but grace and truth came through Jesus Christ" (John 1:17). Jesus called his living water "the gift of God" (John 4:10) and made the gospel challenging enough for a rocket scientist, yet simple enough for a child: "For God so loved the world that He gave His only begotten Son" (John 3:16).

Can God be any clearer that the gospel is infinitely more an announcement of his commitment to us than it will ever be about our commitment to him?

Why, then, do we routinely bypass God's power and concoct a pseudo-salvation mixed with even a speck of human achievement?

Because humans are legalists to the core.

Inconsistencies

Traditional clichés, such as "give your life to Christ" and "commit your life/heart/self to Christ," obviously invert the gospel arrow. So do more insidious terms, like "ask Jesus into your heart/life"—a verbal shortcut that leaves the twin truths of human depravity and Calvary's all-sufficiency in the dust.

I want to pause here long enough to say that God grants salvation to those who turn to Christ, the crucified Savior, regardless of the language they use. Even if that language muddies the waters of grace. Even if it's legalistic. Turning to Christ in faith is all it takes.

Even so, our task is to keep the good news good news, and traditional legalism struggles with that.

Neo-legalism is no different.

One widely read author connects the gospel invitation with giving up everything we possess. Is that the price of redemption?

I spoke with a young, faux-hawked, frosty-haired suburban pastor to find out how he invited people to be saved. He said he didn't. "We're all on a journey," he said. "I'm just inviting people on a journey with Jesus." This is true as far as it goes, but it stops short. It leaves out the best stuff, the Cross/Resurrection stuff. It easily slides into a crossless Christ and a Christless gospel.

A popular neo-discipleship manual says absolutely nothing about the death of Christ in its chapter titled "The Gospel." The authors instead focus on the Kingdom of God in the world. Good stuff, but where's the Cross?

When preachers declare, "There is no salvation without surrender," I want to say, "Yes, but only if you're talking about the great surrender the Savior made in giving up his life."

When they preach, "There is no life without death," I shudder to think they mean any death other than Christ's.

When they announce, "There is no believing without committing," I want to shout that if salvation depends on my commitment for even a nanosecond, I'm doomed. I can't even commit to a diet. If you want to see commitment, look at Christ.

The effect of these statements is to shift the burden of salvation onto the seeker's stooped shoulders. The instant we do that, we diminish the work of Christ and crush the hope out of every frightened human heart.

The gospel offers free salvation precisely because Jesus paid full price. His yoke is easy and his burden light because he already did all the heavy lifting.

To impose obedience, self-improvement, Kingdom building, or radical commitment is to pile on a load no human can bear. Lost people can't commit their lives to Christ; they have no lives. Nor do they have a "commitment organ," spiritually speaking. They can't turn the knob from cold to lukewarm to hot, because their spiritual flame has fizzled in the icy waters of depravity.

I'm all for preaching passion in our lives, but we must never let our passion for Christ eclipse the Passion of Christ. The gospel is not the tale of moral success stories made Christian. It is the story of a Savior who "did not come to improve the improvable"; he "came to raise the dead."[4]

Neo-legalism's distorted gospel sprouts from an emphasis on the life and teachings of Christ at the expense of his death and Resurrection. It offers a life to emulate, more than a death to appropriate. Both are essential, but the death is foundational; the superstructure of Christian living grows no taller than the substructure of cross-centered grace.

"The very first message of the gospel," writes Harry Ironside, "is the story of the vicarious atonement of Christ. He did not come to tell men how to live in order that they might save themselves; He did not come to save men by living His beautiful life. That, apart from His death, would never have saved one poor sinner."[5]

You can shout "Amen!" or click wine glasses—whichever applies.

Just How Radical?

Let's suppose that faith alone in Christ alone is insufficient grounds for salvation. Let's suppose the Bible requires some form of human compliance. Here's my question: *How much of the Bible must a person believe and obey in order to be adopted into God's family and receive eternal life?*

How many pages of Scripture? How many of its commands? How many good works? How many bottles of water distributed? How many duties performed? How many rituals? If salvation is a journey, how many steps must I take before God makes me his own?

Just how radical must I be?

The neo-legalist might argue, "We preach grace, not works. We're not legalists. We know a person isn't saved by good works, or surrender, or obedience, or commitment, or anything like that. But you do have to be willing to do all those things."

Really?

Doesn't that just shove the question back one layer: Just how radically willing must I be to be radically committed?

The Pharisees of Jesus' day had a ready answer: *an entire life of entire obedience to the entire law of God.* Josephus, a Pharisee and historian who lived in Jesus' day, explained the way of salvation in terms of moral consistency. To him, the way to God looked like a tightrope. One slip, and *SPLAT!* No safety net in sight.

> *He who hath at first lived a virtuous life, but*
> *towards the latter end falls into vice, these labors*
> *by him before endured shall be altogether vain*
> *and unprofitable, even as in a play, brought to*
> *an ill catastrophe. Whosoever shall have lived*
> *wickedly and luxuriously may repent; however,*
> *there will be need of much time to conquer an evil*
> *habit, and even after repentance his whole life*
> *must be guarded with great care and diligence.*[6]

Has there ever been a clearer case of Grace Deficit Disorder? No wonder Jesus withstood the Pharisees to their faces. Once we crack open the door to *works salvation*, where do we stop? When can we ever rest on the assurance of sins forgiven and heaven gained?

Where's the good news? I meet so many faithful Christians who never feel they've done enough. They beat themselves up. They doubt their worthiness. They have no clue of their exalted status in grace. They've been pecked almost to death by legalists. They have as much chance of making it across legalism's tightrope in one piece as of winning the lottery, and they'd rather bet on the lottery.

The Pharisees in every generation invariably reach the same conclusion: *if salvation requires human effort before an impeccable deity, then that effort must be perfect, total, and unending.* Religion's demands are relentless. Paul reached the same conclusion: "I testify again to every man who becomes circumcised that he is a debtor to keep the whole law" (Galatians 5:3). So did James: "Whoever shall keep the whole law, and yet stumble in one point, he is guilty of all" (James 2:10).

Let me know how that works for you.

The gospel never lays the burden of whole-Bible obedience on anybody's shoulders for salvation. There is a simple subset of truths, an irreducible minimum, that a seeker must hear and respond to in order to be saved. In every generation, Christians have articulated this gospel in terms their generation can understand.

Here's the formulation I use, following a simple pattern of ABC.

The Gospel of Grace

A stands for Admit: I admit I desperately need God, but I am not worthy of him. That's because, deep inside, I'm a dirty, rotten scoundrel. God is too high (holy), and I'm too low (depraved) for us to get together. The barrier between us slays me; it's hopelessly gigantic, "so high I can't get over it; so low, I can't get under it; so wide, I can't get around it."[7] I'm a sinner, and I need a Savior. I admit it.

B stands for Believe: I believe Jesus shed his blood, dying on the cross and rising again, to reconcile me to God. I believe he died as my substitute, satisfying in full God's righteous demands against my sins. When he rose, he conquered sin, death, hell, and Satan, demolishing the barrier between God and me, once for all. Even though I don't understand how it all works, I believe Jesus Christ is my way to God for time and eternity.

C stands for Choose: I choose to trust in Christ as my only hope. I choose to receive him, to embrace him, and to believe in him as my own. As best as I can, I'm asking God, because of Christ, to forgive my sins, and to make me his child.

> *As many as received Him, to them He gave the right to become children of God, to those who believe in His name: who were born, not of blood, nor of the will of the flesh, nor of the will of man, but of God. (John 1:12–13)*

I don't care how you formulate the gospel, as long as you make Christ crucified the centerpiece. Any old legalist can concoct salvation by human effort. That's why it's so prevalent. But a gospel that is all grace? Rare indeed. Search the annals of religious history—search any culture, any tribe, any part of the world—and you will never find a gospel of pure grace with all the arrows pointing downward.

Works? Yes. Sacrifice? Yes. Obedience? Yes. Ritual? Yes. Service? Yes. Self-improvement? Yes. Giving stuff to God and/or your fellow human? Yes.

Terminal GDD in every case.

But a gospel in which God himself bears the entire burden to reconcile us to himself and to qualify us for heaven? Nobody offers this but the Father of our Lord Jesus Christ. He cornered the market on grace before the foundation of the world.

That is the gospel. That is the irreducible minimum of salvation.

B-B-But What About. . . ?

I know, I know. I wrote "irreducible minimum" and your inner Pharisee blew a gasket. He's probably clawing the walls of your soul this very minute, clamoring for at least a semblance of "balance."

"This author's a libertine!" your inner Pharisee says. "He's giving license to sin! He's making salvation into fire insurance! He's preaching cheap grace! *Irreducible minimum?* That's the whole problem with the church today! People looking for the minimum! Burn him at the stake."

Whoa. . . I understand you. I *was* you. In many ways, I still am. I understand your concern. Too many nominal Christians, not enough sold-out Christ followers. I'm with you. I share that concern.

How will we fix it?

Or, better yet, how did God fix it?

When God wanted to pry the born-again human heart out of its fixation with itself, and into sold-out dedication to him, what lever did he use?

He used the mercies of God.

Here, I'll show you.

> *I beseech you therefore, brethren, by the mercies of God, that you present your bodies a living sacrifice, holy, acceptable to God, which is your reasonable service. (Romans 12:1)*

Notice, God does not get Christians to straighten up and fly right by mashing together salvation and radical commitment.

All that does is add *works* to the equation way too soon, still absent the power of God.

If, however, we start with grace—not leniency, but true grace—we get a free salvation, courtesy of the shed blood of Christ. We get a salvation that is all God and all grace. We get a salvation that brings maximum glory to God, as its author and finisher.

Plus, as a bonus, we get Christ followers who are so smitten with such mercies that they gladly present themselves to God with a humble, "Here am I."

When I fell in love with my wife-to-be, nobody had to scare me into bringing her flowers. I gladly endured the long commute to her house—routinely sixty minutes or more in Chicago's rush hour traffic. I looked forward to our times together. We built a relationship, not out of obligation, but out of love.

Maybe that's always been God's desire for us. We are a people perpetually "beseeched by the mercies of God."

Mercies of God first.

Presenting ourselves to God second.

All attempts to scold, frighten, bribe, or shame people into doing good stuff for God will crash and burn, and deservedly so. We can't make Christians good by threatening to withhold final salvation.

That is not the gospel. That is GDD.

Dear neo-legalist leader: quit bending the gospel out of shape just because you're worried that professing Christians won't rush to change the world. Have a little faith.

Dear traditional legalist leader: quit fretting over casual attire at church; your convert's salvation will survive.

When we start with grace, stick with grace, and finish with grace, we get grateful, assured, confident Christ followers. . . with world service, giving back, and paying it forward on top of the deal. I know, it doesn't always work that way, but quit blaming grace.

"The gift of God is eternal life in Christ Jesus our Lord" (Romans 6:23). "Believe on the Lord Jesus Christ, and you will be saved" (Acts 16:31).

It's that simple.

Don't let the clichés trip you up.

CHAPTER 3

LORDSHIP

You say, Satan, that God is perfectly righteous and the Avenger of all iniquity. I confess it; but I add another property of His righteousness which you have left aside: Since He is righteous, He is satisfied with having been paid once. You say next that I have infinite iniquities which deserve eternal death. I confess it; but I add what you have maliciously omitted: The iniquities which are in me have been very amply avenged and punished in Jesus Christ who has borne the judgment of God in my place.
THEODORE BEZA (1500s)

How about making Jesus Lord and Master of your life?

The 1990s saw a spate of articles and books debating what came to be called the lordship controversy. The question was whether a person's salvation required receiving Christ as Savior only, or as both Savior and Lord, with Lord meaning something like a master to obey.

The question is much older, of course, than this generation. In 1959, John Stott squared off against Everett F. Harrison in *Eternity* magazine in a pair of articles titled "Must Christ Be

Lord to Be Savior?" with Stott arguing pro and Harrison con.[8]

Going back to the fifteenth century, we find similar questions swirling around the precise nature of faith, assurance, the gospel, and salvation.[9]

In modern times, camps have formed around each opinion, with evangelical heavyweights on each side. Leading the lordship charge have been John MacArthur, John Stott, J. I. Packer, A. W. Tozer, James Montgomery Boice, and numerous Reformed/Calvinist luminaries. Recent proponents include best-selling authors Francis Chan, Kyle Idleman, and David Platt.[10]

The Savior-only side boasted Charles C. Ryrie, Lewis Sperry Chafer, Zane Hodges, Charles Stanley, Chuck Swindoll, and many within institutions such as Dallas Theological Seminary and Moody Bible Institute. More recently, Tullian Tchividjian, Charlie Bing, Andrew Farley, Steve McVey, Paul Ellis, the Free Grace Alliance, and the Grace Evangelical Society have added their voices.

Where's the beef?

The lordship side requires repentance from sins and obedience to God as essential components of saving faith. Faith and works, for them, can't be separated.

For example, John MacArthur has declared obedience to be "synonymous with faith."[11] He says obedience is "indivisibly wrapped up in the idea of believing."[12] His 1988 book *The Gospel According to Jesus* became the mother ship of the modern lordship movement. This position, often aligned with Calvinism and modern Reformed theology, is often called the lordship position.

When I was a young Christian, starved for solid Bible

teaching, it was John MacArthur who came to my rescue through his recordings and books. This makes it hard for me to critique his position, and I do it with all humility, love, and affection.

Savior-only critics swarmed MacArthur's book immediately. Articulating a position that some call *free grace*, they traced their view through Luther and Calvin all the way back to Jesus and Paul. I believe the case goes back to Moses, but that's beyond my scope.

In case it isn't clear, I count myself among the free grace tribe. Advocates of free grace point out that any mingling of works with faith within the gospel message nullifies faith and makes grace no longer grace. It returns Christianity to pre-Reformation legalism and dresses medieval salvation-by-works in modern garb.

Free grace must be a term invented by the department of redundancy department. What other grace can there be? It is no accident the word *gratis*, which means free, doubles as the Latin word for grace.

Under the teaching of free grace, a person receives Jesus as Savior first and subsequently grows to respond to him as Lord in obedience and holiness.

Faith and works are not synonymous, and to suggest they are dissolves each into a blob of meaninglessness. It also overlooks the many contrasts drawn in Scripture: "Knowing that a man is not justified by the works of the law but by faith in Jesus Christ, even we have believed in Christ Jesus, that we might be justified by faith in Christ and not by the works of the law; for by the works of the law no flesh shall be justified" (Galatians 2:16).

I scratch my head over the claim that faith and works are synonymous, when, to Paul, they were clearly opposites.

The whole thing became a theological cage match when each side accused the other of preaching "another gospel" and the *anathemas* flew (Galatians 1:8–9). While both sides stockpiled books, articles, and conferences in support of their positions, they missed a far more important reality: when it comes to the essential doctrines of our faith, free grace and lordship salvation have far more in common than not. Neither side would question the work of God through proponents of free grace such as Chuck Swindoll or supporters of lordship salvation such as John MacArthur; or through institutions such as Reformed Theological Seminary or Moody Bible Institute. Yes, we have our disagreements, but we're still on the same team.

Both sides preach Christ crucified and risen again.

Both sides uphold the authority of Scripture.

Both sides honor the exclusivity of the gospel—there's no other way than Jesus.

Both sides teach the absolute necessity of new birth.

Both sides seek to exclude human works from the equation of salvation.

Both sides sing "Amazing Grace" with equal gusto.

Both sides want converts to live holy lives.

Both sides teach the saviorhood of Christ.

Both sides teach the lordship of Christ.

Both sides could sign each other's doctrinal statements, except, perhaps, for the statement on saving faith. And this is exactly the point of contention: How is a person born again?

The controversy has cooled to a quiet simmer in recent

years. This is partly because a tidal wave of theological indifference has swept over the church, and partly because most people assume the lordship side won.

I don't think either side won. Whether we say, "Make Jesus your Lord," or, "Make Jesus your Savior," the average Christian sees little distinction—and non-Christians see no distinction at all.

So who won the lordship wars?

Biblical illiteracy won. Marginal theology has been enshrined in clichés repeated by both sides with little effect: give up everything you have, make Jesus your Savior, make Jesus your Lord, ask Jesus into your heart/life, just pray this prayer. Lordship salvation is still labeled as legalism, and free grace is still labeled as cheap grace, so it's hard to see how either side really got its point across.

One Jesus Christ

Another staunch advocate of lordship salvation, A. W. Tozer, made his position abundantly clear:

> *I must be frank in my feeling that a notable heresy
> has come into being throughout our evangelical
> Christian circles—the widely accepted concept
> that we humans can choose to accept Christ only
> because we need Him as Savior and we have the
> right to postpone our obedience to Him as Lord as
> long as we want to! . . .*
>
> *You cannot believe on a half-Christ. We take
> Him for what He is—the anointed Saviour and
> Lord who is King of kings and Lord of all lords!* [13]

First, if I can accomplish even the remotest fraction of what Tozer accomplished in his remarkable ministry, I will be a happy man. I love his books, his exalted view of God, and his influence for Christ. I've even spoken from his historic pulpit. So I hesitate to take him on. But this statement requires an answer.

By mischaracterizing the free grace position, Tozer has slain a straw man. And by dropping the H-bomb (heresy) on sincere students of God's Word, on an issue where reasonable Christians disagree, he risks giving the onlooking world a cause to be skeptical of the gospel.

Here are three answers to Tozer's critique, and to lordship salvation in general:

1. Christ is undivided in his person, but divided in his offices.

When we receive Jesus Christ, we receive both the Lord and the Savior. I heartily support Tozer's affirmation that we can't split Christ in two. He is undivided in his person. But free grace never calls seekers to believe on *half* of Christ. We don't make him Lord; he is Lord. And as our Savior, he delivers us from fallenness and sin. As Lord, he is both deity and master.

For the record, I confess Jesus Christ as Lord. Every Christian is called to respond to him as such. We should obey, fear, and follow him. We must submit, surrender, and give all allegiance to him. Christians should be holy. We shouldn't sin. I know of no one who teaches Tozer's idea of postponing obedience "as long as we want to."

Even so, the inconvenient truth remains that obedience to Christ's lordship is utterly impossible for people who don't have Christ. It would constitute a works-based salvation if anybody were to preach it to them. Even after we're saved, any obedience that actually counts with God remains impossible apart from abiding in Christ.

To demand obedience to Christ's lordship from a person without Christ's power is a surefire way to beat up a sensitive soul.

What do you do with a Savior? Receive him. Accept him. Thank him. Believe in him.

What do you do with a Lord? Obey him. Honor him. Follow him.

Christ is not divided in his person or his being. He is, however, divided in his offices, and here is where I part ways with Tozer's statement.

Allow me to illustrate.

In my relationship with my son, I am one father, one person. But at various times I display different aspects of my fatherhood, according to my son's capabilities and needs, and he responds to me in different ways, depending on the situation. Sometimes he responds to me as provider. Sometimes he responds to me as football coach. Sometimes he responds to me as his personal IT department (though that relationship is rapidly reversing). Sometimes he responds to me as disciplinarian, counselor, teacher, jokester, or beast of burden to carry his football gear. In the future, he will respond to me as college adviser and soon-to-be-broke banker.

I love all my offices, all aspects of my relationship with my son. They are part and parcel of being a dad to him. I make completely different demands on him on the football field than I do at the dinner table.

Am I inconsistent by this? No.

Is he inconsistent? No.

In the same way, Jesus Christ is the undivided God-man, leading with different aspects of his being at different times, according to a person's capability and need.

To the woman caught in adultery, he presented himself as the one who refused to condemn. To sisters mourning their brother's death, he showed up as the Resurrection and the Life. To a woman with an unstaunched flow of blood, he was both healer and encourager. To a famished multitude, he was a miracle-working chef, in addition to shepherd, teacher, and friend.[14]

In the Old Testament, he was Moses' burning bush, Ezekiel's wheel within a wheel, and Israel's cloud by day and fire by night. He was a fireproof shield to three men in a furnace, a sinkhole of wrath to rebels, a lamb of rescue to Isaac, and an ark of deliverance to Noah.[15]

He is the devil's destroyer, a proud king's downfall, and a harlot's salvation.[16]

In all this was Christ divided?

No.

Christ's offices are innumerable. Overwhelming, really. No mere mortal can respond to all of Christ all at once, legalistic clichés notwithstanding. If he came at you that way, you'd explode. If you were to encounter him as he truly is—comprehensively, in totality—you'd be devastated beyond recovery. You can't handle the Truth.

The issue is far more complex than simply defining two categories of Savior and Lord.

Who is sufficient for these things?

No one.

So God does what any self-respecting God of all grace would do: he presents himself to each person, in each circumstance, according to that person's capability and need. Is a lost person capable of serving, obeying, or in any way pleasing Christ as Master and Lord? No. Can the spiritually dead bring forth fruit worthy of repentance? No. It's impossible. So God doesn't demand it.

> *And they were greatly astonished, saying among themselves, "Who then can be saved?" But Jesus looked at them and said, "With men it is impossible, but not with God; for with God all things are possible." (Mark 10:26–27)*

What do people who are flailing in an ocean of sin, weighed down by corruption, crushed by despair, utterly depraved, broken, beyond hope, and about to drown in eternal perdition really need?

A savior.

They need a rescuing hand to deliver them from death. As that saving hand stretches forth to rescue, is it even conceivable that the Savior runs through a list of post-deliverance "terms and conditions" before he takes hold?

There is but one command for people who are lost: *Believe on the Lord Jesus Christ and you will be saved.*

Jesus Christ saves the lost and he commands the saved. He can exercise no practical lordship in our lives—other than condemnation, conviction, and revelation—unless he saves us first. We then have a lifetime to discover that we will never find a better king than Jesus.

2. Faith is non-meritorious.

Put yourself in God's shoes for a moment. You, the Infinite One, are going to offer a magnificent salvation to fallen and finite humans. You have determined that this salvation will come as a gift. Among other purposes, you wish to show forth your grace for all the ages to come. So you design a pure, free, unmerited, unearned, unrecompensed gift of unmixed charity. You will not tally merit badges before bestowing this gift. You will factor in no calculation of human worthiness whatsoever. No works. No rituals. Nothing.

In your sovereign counsels, you determine not to force anyone into this salvation. They must respond freely to your gracious offer in order to seal the deal.

What response will you require?

Immediately, you rule out good works, or else grace is no longer grace.

Along with good works, out goes religious observance, for the same reason. No human fingerprints can mar this testament of grace. Not one molecule of boasting can be allowed.

What can a fallen, finite person possibly do so that all the merit rests in the giver and none in the receiver? What human response suits this situation?

Faith. Only faith.

I can't tell you how many times I've dealt with the objection that faith is "doing something" to be saved. That's not exactly true. Faith is undoing something. It's giving up self-effort, self-performance, and self-salvation. Faith turns from self to Christ and says, "You're the man."

This makes faith an *un*work. With faith, we acknowledge our own *absence* of merit, so that we might rely on the merit of another.

Grace seeks faith like a heat-seeking missile. In salvation, the act of faith is a raw admission of helplessness. It is abject humility reaching out empty hands. By exercising faith, you acknowledge your inability so that you might rest on Christ's ability.

When God chose to require faith, he selected the only possible human response that points away from self. He chose the one human response that leaves grace intact, unsmudged by our self-promoting fingerprints. He chose the one and only healing balm for the miseries of Grace Deficit Disorder.

If grace means God does all the work, then only faith can mesh with grace. Religion can't, because religion requires human performance and ritual. Law can't, because law requires human obedience. A system of morality or good works can't mesh with grace, because grace excludes human achievement. Only faith, with empty hands laying hold of Christ's finished work, can properly mesh with grace, in which God does all the work. Grace is faith's docking station.

The greatest problem in lordship preaching is what seekers hear. No matter how many qualifiers the preacher adds, the seeker hears works. The seeker hears a litany of duties that seem utterly out of reach. Instead of "just as I am," the listener hears "just as you aren't."

Neither free grace advocates nor lordship advocates do anybody any favors when they say, "Faith works." Technically, it doesn't. *Christ* works. Faith unites us to him. Our hope is not in salvation; our hope is in Christ. Our hope is not getting saved; our hope is in Christ. Our hope is not in praying a prayer, walking an aisle, improving our morality, or raising our hand. Our hope is always and ever and only in the One who loved us and gave his life for us.

Horatius Bonar, a nineteenth-century Scottish preacher, offers a helpful description of faith:

> *Faith is not Christ, nor the cross of Christ. Faith is not the blood, nor the sacrifice; it is not the altar, nor the laver, nor the mercy-seat, nor the incense. It does not work, but accepts a work done ages ago; it does not wash, but leads us to the fountain opened for sin and uncleanness. It does not create; it merely links us to that new thing which was created when the "everlasting righteousness" was brought in. (Daniel 9:24)*[17]

3. Grace is not cheap.

There's no easier torpedo to fire at the free grace position than that of "cheap grace." When the allegation comes from a heroic pastor, martyred while taking on the satanic forces of Hitler's Nazism, the response becomes exceedingly delicate. Dietrich Bonhoeffer stands with those valiant warriors who gave their all for Christ. I count myself among the ranks of Bonhoeffer's admirers, even as I state my respectful disagreement to a particular statement of his against free grace.

> *Cheap grace means the justification of sin without the justification of the sinner. Grace alone does everything, they say, and so everything can remain as it was before. "All for sin could not atone." The world goes on in the same old way, and we are still sinners "even in the best life" as*

Luther said. Well, then, let the Christian live like the rest of the world, let him model himself on the world's standards in every sphere of life, and not presumptuously aspire to live a different life under grace from his old life under sin. . . . Cheap grace is the grace we bestow on ourselves.

Cheap grace is the preaching of forgiveness without requiring repentance, baptism without church discipline, Communion without confession . . . . Cheap grace is grace without discipleship, grace without the cross, grace without Jesus Christ, living and incarnate.[18]

As powerful as Bonhoeffer's writing is, every line merits thoughtful analysis. For example, no respectable free grace teacher I know of advocates "the justification of sin." Nor do we teach "the justification of the sinner," in Bonhoeffer's sense of rationalizing a sinful lifestyle. By misrepresenting free grace teachings, Bonhoeffer's critique slays a straw man.

Likewise, his play on "grace alone" is troubling: "Grace alone does everything, they say. . . ." When the church says "grace alone," we are merely echoing the great Reformation motto, *sola gratia.* The initiative and work belong to God alone. The power, energy, election, and labor are all his. And yes, grace alone *does* accomplish everything required for salvation, as Christians of all stripes must say, or else Christ's death was not enough.

Without "grace alone," the cross has no scandal. The gospel has no power. The cross has no meaning. If salvation is not by grace alone, then Christianity becomes just one of many equivalent world religions, varying only in the type and number of works they require.

Without sola gratia, Christ died in vain, and reaching him is an exercise in the survival of the fittest.

Without sola gratia, the most beautiful, life-giving, hope-producing revelation ever given to humanity fades into oblivion.

No doubt Bonhoeffer would affirm sola gratia, but perhaps only after expanding *gratia* beyond it roots to its fruits.

When Bonhoeffer labels as presumptive a Christian's aspiration "to live a different life under grace from his old life under sin," he misses the free grace point entirely, deepening the straw man fallacy. Apart from Calvary's unmixed grace, there simply is no gateway out of the life of sin and into a life of holiness.

Whatever else grace may "require," it cannot include legalistic forms of repentance. It can require only a repentance that empties its hands of the very commodity Bonhoeffer argues we must offer. As soon as we lump together saving faith with behavioral repentance, baptism, church discipline, Communion, confession, and discipleship, we empty both *grace* and *faith* of any meaning. We unravel the Reformation motto, *Fides est fiducia* (Faith is trust).[19]

Perhaps influenced by Karl Barth, Bonhoeffer's writing on grace reveals a tendency toward paradox.[20] For example, he ends this section on free grace by pulling the rug out from underneath his own argument: cheap grace, he says, is "grace without the cross, grace without Jesus Christ, living and incarnate." In this, he echoes what free grace proponents have been saying all along. Later, he swims to the deep end of the paradoxical pool:

Such grace is costly because it calls us to follow,
and it is grace because it calls us to follow Jesus
Christ. It is costly because it costs a man his life,
and it is grace because it gives a man the only true
life. It is costly because it condemns sin, and grace
because it justifies the sinner. Above all, it is costly
because it cost God the life of his Son: "ye were
bought at a price," and what has cost God much
cannot be cheap for us.[21]

He correctly sets the word *"costly"* in opposition to the word
"grace." I wish he had stayed with that. One person's love of
paradox is another person's eloquent confusion. By using
the word costly in a number of different senses in the same
paragraph, Bonhoeffer makes his argument tough to follow.
The central difficulty lies in his failure to state who exactly
pays the cost, and what it consists of. And that oversight stems
from erroneously conflating salvation with discipleship, and
justification with sanctification.

Is following Christ in a life of obedience the *cost* we pay?
Isn't that salvation by works?

Is giving our lives to God—a phrase that inverts grace's
arrows and bypasses Calvary altogether—the *cost* we pay? Are
we to barter one life for another? What does it even mean
to "give one's life," but either to die or to obey, in both cases
obliterating a free salvation?

Bonhoeffer says, "Grace is costly because it condemns sin,"
to which we say, "Amen." But who was condemned? If it was
Christ alone, then hallelujah. If it is the disciple, we cannot
see how that squares with Scripture (Romans 8:1; John 3:36).

The problem running throughout this passage from Bonhoeffer is not just paradox. It is outright contradiction, as exhibited by this beautiful sentence: "Above all, it is costly because it cost God the life of his Son." Why not start and stop right there? Isn't this the true "cost of discipleship"? To then add, "What has cost God much cannot be cheap for us," evaporates the argument into a misty haze. Is the blood-bought grace of our Lord Jesus Christ up for sale?

This illuminates a profound irony that has yet to be answered by those who fire the charge of "cheap grace": it's one thing to require a *cost* for salvation; it's another thing to presume we can actually afford to pay it.

Who cheapens grace? Is it not those whose price tag lies within human reach?

Is it not those who trade Christ's blood-bought blessings for a price denominated in human performance?

Is it not those who tell lost souls to look to themselves to somehow balance the divine ledger?

What is the cost of discipleship?

More than you can afford.

Christ's first task when dealing with sinners was to slay their hope in themselves. He adapted his message to the attitude of the one he faced.

Of those who thought they had nothing, Jesus demanded nothing, because abject humility needs no adjustment to mesh perfectly with grace—for example, the woman taken in adultery (John 8:11), the sinful woman of the city (Luke 7:37–50), blind Bartimaeus (Mark 10:46–52), and the thief on the cross (Luke 23:40–43).

Of those who thought they had something to give, Jesus

demanded everything and more, but only to show them their own bankruptcy—for example, the rich young ruler (Luke 18:22–23), the party poopers too self-satisfied for the great feast (Luke 14:16–22), those who counted the cost and thought they could actually afford it (Luke 14:28–35, where the punch line says their capital was just a pile of dung). These hard requirements were never the "Gospel according to Jesus." They stand forever as the impossibly high price tag on an out-of-reach treasure, for dummies too arrogant to admit their insufficiency.

To say there is a price is one thing. To say we can pay it is another.

The only way to cheapen grace is to propose a price that humans can actually afford to pay.

The Acid Test

For either camp—lordship or free grace—the acid test remains the same. The great question of salvation hinges not on human behavior or a litany of obeyed imperatives. It is always and forever the simple question, Where is your hope for eternity? Are you counting on Christ or on something else? Are you counting on Christ plus nothing, or Christ plus something?

Is Christ crucified a portion of your salvation plan, or is he everything?

When God asks you to point to one good reason why you should be forgiven—why you should be his child, why you should be saved, why you should go to heaven—where will you point? Will you point to yourself? To your faithfulness?

To your submission, surrender, commitment, or love?

Or will you point away from yourself to the one who is seated at God's right hand, whose hands and feet bear the prints of the nails, whose brow bears the scars from the thorns, and whose face bears a smile of acceptance?

Point.

To.

Jesus.

Christ.

The saving grace in any gospel presentation is simply a constant return to the Cross. Whether I'm reading great writers such as Bonhoeffer, MacArthur, Tchividjian, Lutzer, Piper, Swindoll, Spurgeon, Tozer—who fall on one side or the other of the debate—the glory is always in the Cross. These are writers who make frequent references to Christ crucified, and therein lies the explosive power of the gospel. There pulses the heartbeat of grace. The Cross covers all our sins, preaching and otherwise.

Scandalous

I've come to believe the only way to properly teach grace is to scandalize the hearer. When a teacher does it right, people get indignant. And by "people" I mean *legalists*. And by "legalists" I mean you—and me. And everyone else who still doesn't quite grasp how desperately mired in the sewer of depravity we really are apart from Christ.

In Romans 6:1, Paul asks, "Shall we continue in sin that grace may abound?"

For five full chapters, he has laid out a rich feast of grace.

He has described the courtroom drama of sin and salvation in all its guts and glory. He has explored the riches of Christ's cross from every conceivable angle. He has magnified grace and shown faith—however imperfect—to be the sufficient pipeline by which we receive it. Good works have been wiped off the table. So has all human righteousness whatsoever. Ditto for rituals and rites.

All that's left are the sparkling gospel of pure grace and the bloodied Savior who purchased it.

Having taught grace for five chapters, Paul anticipates the objection of Romans 6:1: "What are you saying, all this grace means we can sin with impunity? All this grace means sin doesn't matter anymore? Why not just grab the fire insurance and then do whatever we want? You're giving false hope! You're cheapening the gospel! Aren't you giving license to sin, you libertine?!"

Shall we continue in sin that grace may abound?

I have come to realize that grace is supposed to produce those kinds of questions. That's how we know we're teaching it right. When we've scandalized the hearer. When we've agitated the legalist. When we've evoked the charge of "antinomianism." And when those who insist they can buy heaven frown and walk away—or cry, "Crucify him!"

A visceral hatred of grace is a symptom of nearly terminal GDD.

Jesus Christ, who is both Savior and Lord, invites you to encounter him as Savior so that he might activate all your potentialities to follow him as Lord.

The old couplet says, "Nothing in my hand I bring / Simply to thy Cross I cling."

True enough.

But the deeper truth is that Jesus is the one who is clinging to you, and that's all the comfort a frail heart will ever need.

CHAPTER 4

NEO-MISHNAH

Make no laws upon the saints
where Christ hath not made any.[22]
WALTER CRADOCK

Long before the days of Jesus, Judaism birthed a system of regulations beyond the Law of Moses. These regulations, called the Oral Torah, stood like surly bodyguards beside the biblical law itself. They "protected" God's people from accidentally breaking the real law. Later generations recorded these rules and called them the Mishnah.

For example, while the Law of Moses prohibited work on the Sabbath, the Mishnah prohibited even holding a tool on the Sabbath—say, an ax or hammer—lest one accidentally swing it and break the real law. The Jews compared this to building a fence around the law. One rabbi wrote,

The Torah is conceived as a garden and its precepts as precious plants. Such a garden is fenced round for the purpose of obviating willful or even unintended

> *damage. Likewise, the precepts of the Torah were to*
> *be "fenced" round with additional inhibitions that*
> *should have the effect of preserving the original*
> *commandments from trespass.*[23]

These regulations came to be called *traditions* (Greek, *paradosis*). Over the centuries, the traditions multiplied like rabbits on steroids. Whereas the entire Old Testament fits in a single volume, the Mishnah requires three sturdy bookshelves. This "fence around the law" morphed into a mode of ultra-obedience to God.

I sympathize with the motives behind fencing the law. When my kids were little, I was glad that swimming pools had fences around them.

But God's laws are not swimming pools, and they don't need fences. That, at least, was Jesus' opinion. He rebuked the Pharisees for promoting their traditions above God's Word. "All too well you reject the commandment of God, that you may keep your tradition [paradosis]" (Mark 7:9). In other words, ultra-obedience is disobedience.

By their ultra-obedience to the commandments of God, the Pharisees wound up rejecting the commandments of God. Ironic, huh? (If you grew up as a fundamentalist or a legalist, you may be nodding your head real fast right now.)

Here's an example of how ultra-obedience or "fencing" God's commandments works.

The Bible doesn't stutter when it prohibits adultery (Exodus 20:14). It's a good law because it's God's law.

God's law, however, does not prohibit mixed-gender swimming. That policy might be wise in some contexts. It might make for excellent personal scruples. Yet it is not and never will be God's inspired Word.

My friend Donny grew up in a pastor's home in what he calls a legalistic church. His church prohibited "mixed bathing" and required women who wanted to swim to wear full-length dresses and be quarantined from the men. Donny rebelled, like so many other victims of legalism, hopping into the porn industry and becoming one of the nation's leading producers (until Jesus captured his heart).

Could God be saying that his Word is perfect, and when we add to it, we rile up people's dark side?

When a member of the youth group I attended as a kid wanted to date our Sunday school teacher's daughter, the father/teacher required the suitor to first pass a written Bible quiz. For real.

Question 1: What does 1 Corinthians 7:1 say about touching a woman?

Answer (from the beautiful, old King James Version of that day): "It is good for a man not to touch a woman." Some more recent translations recognize this as meaning voluntary celibacy; the NIV reads, "It is good for a man not to have sexual relations with a woman."

But that's not what it meant in my little church. It meant no touching under any circumstances. We erected our own fence around God's laws—enforced with as much energy as God's law itself.

A twenty-something contractor was working in my house, when, in conversation, he discovered I was a pastor. He smiled, held out his arms, and said, "I'm a Christian, too, see?" I couldn't see what he was talking about. Two arms, two sleeves covering them, no tattoos peeking out at the wrists, nothing to see. Just arms.

I asked what he was showing me.

He said, "I'm wearing long sleeves." He said his pastor told him men should always wear long sleeves so their potentially sexy arms wouldn't cause young women to stumble.

Seriously.

Sometime later, I heard he went to prison for sexual crimes. Apparently, covering his arms had not transformed his heart.

Another One Bites the Dust

The whole wagon train goes off the cliff when the victims of legalism come to embrace it as their own. That's what I did. I became the cleanest-cut American Boy Scout you could imagine. I didn't dance, drink, smoke, swear (much), lust (much), fornicate, steal, or cheat on tests. I helped in children's ministry, played in the church band, and attended prayer meetings. I even helped start early-morning prayer meetings on the steps of my massive Chicago high school. My fence around the law beat the next guy's by a mile.

This all would have been great, I suppose, if in the process I hadn't become a self-righteous weasel. I was better than my peers, and I knew it. How could God not be impressed with me? My upward arrows were solid gold.

But when moral performance becomes our focus, the good news gets swamped by bad news. For me, the bad news was an unrelenting need to perform. Maintaining that squeaky-clean image took its toll. I didn't know it, but Grace Deficit Disorder had burrowed deep within my tender psyche.

I loved Jesus, but it felt like he was wearing me out.

What about neo-legalism? As a more up-to-date Christian culture has turned away from rules and taboos, has it embraced another set of extra-biblical requirements without realizing it?

The Prime Coordinator

My grandparents migrated to America from Italy. Registered at Ellis Island, they found their way to Chicago, brought my dad into the world, and—*bada-bing*—here I am. We spent most of my childhood Sundays at Grandma and Grandpa's house, feasting on homemade pasta, soup, and roast beef and crashing on the sofa while the grown-ups watched football.

My grandparents' house smelled deliciously Italian. I can't catch a whiff of Italian cooking today without being instantly transported to lazy afternoons and a full belly in Grandma's kitchen.

That delicious aroma, however, was completely lost on my grandparents. What to me smelled Italian, to them smelled normal. If I had said, "Wow, Grandma, your house smells great," she would've asked, "What smell are you talking about?" That's because cultural values become transparent to those who hold them. Greeks don't dance to *Greek* music; they dance to *music*. Southerners don't make *Southern* fried chicken; they make *fried chicken*.

Likewise, legalists and neo-legalists don't impose extra-biblical standards; they just expect normal behavior—as they define it. This makes their legalism extra stealthy. What's so bad about expecting normal?

Madeleine L'Engle, in her award-winning sci-fi fantasy *A*

Wrinkle in Time, describes life on the horrid planet Camazotz. Citizens there displayed a frightening conformity to one another. All the children bounced their balls to the same inaudible rhythm. All the houses looked the same. All the mothers summoned their children for dinner at precisely the same moment.[24]

Behind the Stepford-like uniformity lay a disembodied brain called the Prime Coordinator, which emitted an invisible, inaudible, hypnotic pulse, coordinating all activities on the planet, including everyone's heartbeat.

One boy who broke the rhythm by dropping his ball was later seen in a chamber with pulsating lights, being reconditioned to the norm.

Reminds me of some churches I've known.

Reminds me of some of the legalistic systems that Jesus blasted.

For younger adults, driven in large measure by a need for acceptance, cultural norms substitute as the Prime Coordinator.

Assimilate or perish.

Whether it's the bun-topped Prime Coordinator of a traditional church looking down her pinched nose in disapproval, or the latte-sipping Prime Coordinator of a neo-legalistic church snickering with his friends over your *MacArthur Study Bible*, what's the difference? Either way, anyone who doesn't assimilate is assigned a spot on the periphery—and feels it. That's one way we can be victimized by other people's Grace Deficit Disorder.

And our own GDD answers with our own brand of insecurity.

The scary thing is that we hardly realize it's happening.

We're blind to our own tyranny of coolness.

Whether it's the right tattoos, the coolest piercings, the ever-evolving stylings of rabbinical-style facial hair, or a general disdain for Christ-followers labeled "unloving" just for standing by their theology, neo-legalism remains painfully blind to its own paradosis—its own extra-biblical standards. Environmental and social consciousness may be good and holy endeavors, but they're not the linchpins of the gospel. They never will be. Lessening one's carbon footprint, swaying to the latest Christian music, keeping up with hashtags, and loving Jesus while hating the church—none of these are biblically enforceable.

We can be deeply spiritual followers of Christ, and genuinely born again, without holding tightly to any of the values in the neo-legalistic package. But where, then, do we fit in? Where will we find cool friends?

As long as admission to the club requires conformity to extra-biblical standards, we are lost in the vast wasteland of legalism. Without intending to, we've created a neo-Mishnah. We've become blind to our own Grace Deficit Disorder.

The Bible is enough. God doesn't need help. The Spirit of Christ, who superintended the writers of Scripture, did his job flawlessly. Nothing is missing. Nothing should be added. God can stand on his own two literary feet.

There is exactly one legitimate stumbling block between lost people and their Maker: the offense of the Cross. If people balk at a crucified Savior, they'll answer to God for that. Let's make sure we're not adding even the slightest needless stumbling block (Romans 14:13).

That same cross, and the risen, ascended Savior who now

dwells within regenerated hearts, never ceases to be the main thing—indeed, the only thing—needed for a life of holiness and grace.

But God help us if our friends stumble over our self-defined, self-serving demands—whether religious, cultural, or ethical.

If we teach Christians to grow in grace, we won't need to hound them with calls to world service or to holiness; the one who abides in Christ produces much fruit—naturally, in accordance with the life of the Vine.

Life with God starts with grace, ends with grace, and rests on grace in between.

Anything else is needless fine print.

CHAPTER 5

THE GAP

Happy the soul that has been
awed by a view of God's majesty.
A. W. PINK

Whatever God is, he is without measure. Legalists, while paying lip service to God's limitlessness, figure out ways to mash him into their thimble-sized mental frameworks. The result is a schizoid stew in which God is simultaneously *unreachable* by any means and *reachable* by human means. Either way, our view of God is diminished; he is made into something less than infinite—both in his holiness and in his power to forgive.

For the first two decades of my Christian walk, I dreaded the eventual, inevitable "heavenly final exam." I was convinced that God was fully prepared to broadcast my secret sins for the entire universe to see. I pictured myself cowering before the judgment seat, a trembling, naked Italian boy, while God and the angels stared in disgust at my most secret and heinous imaginations.

After making me squirm for a while, the heavenly Father would roll his eyes, his only begotten Son would blush to call me his own, and the Holy Spirit would wag the foam finger of shame, until, with a sigh, the Trinity would grant me grudging entrance to my eternal double-wide. Maybe.

How I dreaded that day!

Without realizing it, I had diminished (in my mind) God's power to forgive.

A parallel tendency, common among neo-legalists in particular, is to shrink God's holiness and grandeur, as evidenced by a skew toward universalism and away from evangelism among younger Christians.[25]

God does not like it when we shrink him.

One time, God instantly fried a guy—who knew better—for acting as if God needed a hand (2 Samuel 6:6–7). I realize that Uzzah's incineration in a book about grace sticks out like dung in a diamond heap, but please bear with me. We do grace no favors by painting a red-hot God in pastel shades of bland tolerance.

The prophets railed against the sin of idolatry. Isaiah leveled blistering sarcasm against anyone foolish enough to chop down a tree in the morning, carve an idol from it in the afternoon, and bow in worship before it at night (Isaiah 40:20–21). There is no such thing as a pocket-sized edition of God.

The writers of Scripture strain human vocabulary in their attempts to depict God's grandeur:

- He is "the High and Lofty One who inhabits eternity" (Isaiah 57:15).

- He sits on a throne, "high and lifted up" (Isaiah 6:1).
- "Before the mountains were brought forth...from everlasting to everlasting," he is God (Psalm 90:2).
- "At His wrath, the earth will tremble" (Jeremiah 10:10).
- "No one is holy like the Lord, for there is none besides You, nor is there any rock like our God" (1 Samuel 2:2).

There is a greatness, a grandeur, and a loftiness to God that overloads the circuits of ordinary mortals who encounter him. The barest glimpse of God's glory made Daniel pass out and get sick for days (Daniel 8:27). "Woe is me, for I am undone!" cried the prophet Isaiah when he "saw the Lord sitting on a throne, high and lifted up" (Isaiah 6:1–5). When John saw a vision of the conquering Savior, he "fell at His feet as dead" (Revelation 1:17). In Exodus 33:22, when the glory of God passed by, God hid Moses in a cleft of a rock and covered him with his hand for protection.

There is simply no way to read Scripture without coming away with the idea that God is exceedingly, abundantly, immeasurably exalted above fallen mortals like us.

In case it isn't obvious, I am bending over backward to highlight the impassible chasm that exists between God's true grace and the fabricated, sentimental, romantic, gooey, mushy, wimpy, anything-goes niceness that the word *grace* has come to imply.

The God we serve is big and dangerous. He is a consuming fire—unquenchable. He plays by nobody's rules but his own. Any God who would command a man (Abraham) to sacrifice his son (Isaac), and who opened up the earth to swallow rebels, is not to be trifled with.

And lest we fall prey to the clichéd delusion that the God of the Old Testament was a God of wrath, but the God of the New Testament ushered in mercy and love, let us pause to flip those switches. Here are five scary New Testament statements on God's wrath, along with five heartwarming Old Testament statements on God's grace.

DIVINE HOLINESS AND WRATH IN THE NEW TESTAMENT

Romans 1:18: *The wrath of God is revealed from heaven against all ungodliness and unrighteousness of men, who suppress the truth in unrighteousness.*

Hebrews 12:29: *Our God is a consuming fire.*

1 Timothy 6:15–16: *He who is the blessed and only Potentate, the King of kings and Lord of lords, who alone has immortality, dwelling in unapproachable light, whom no man has seen or can see.*

Matthew 10:28: *"Do not fear those who kill the body but cannot kill the soul. But rather fear Him who is able to destroy both soul and body in hell."*

Hebrews 10:31: *It is a fearful thing to fall into the hands of the living God.*

Divine Grace and Mercy
in the Old Testament

Isaiah 49:15: *"Can a woman forget her nursing child, And not have compassion on the son of her womb? Surely they may forget, Yet I will not forget you."*

Psalm 86:5: *You, Lord, are good, and ready to forgive, And abundant in mercy to all those who call upon You.*

Psalm 103:2–5: *Bless the Lord, O my soul, And forget not all His benefits: Who forgives all your iniquities, Who heals all your diseases, Who redeems your life from destruction, Who crowns you with lovingkindness [Hebrew hesed = grace] and tender mercies, Who satisfies your mouth with good things, So that your youth is renewed like the eagle's.*

Joel 2:13: *Rend your heart, and not your garments; Return to the Lord your God, For He is gracious and merciful, Slow to anger, and of great kindness; And He relents from doing harm.*

Zephaniah 3:17: *"The Lord your God in your midst, the Mighty One, will save; He will rejoice over you with gladness, He will quiet you with His love, He will rejoice over you with singing."*

The entire Bible is a book of boundless grace that can only be grace when set against the backdrop of a blistering holiness stretching to infinity and beyond.

What's the point?

Simply that human nature is hopelessly addicted to squishing God into a quart-sized baggie. This is part of the GDD syndrome. But despite our best efforts to diminish him, God refuses to not be big.

In the end, that's one of the great secrets of grace. Grace is the force that fills the gap between God's soaring greatness and our bottom-feeding fallenness. Any attempts to lower God will, in effect, suck the amazingness right out of grace.

Likewise with any attempts to elevate the rotten-dumpster works from our sin-tainted hearts. The naked truth remains that our boundless iniquity can only be answered by God's gracious infinity.

Iniquity

An old-time preacher said, "If you knew how much corruption was in my heart, you wouldn't waste your time listening to me." He paused as a chuckle worked through the audience and added, "But that's okay. Because if I knew how much corruption was in your heart, I wouldn't waste my time preaching to you."

I can't claim to speak for you or anybody else, but sometimes my mental arena looks an awful lot like a freakish carnival, worked by scary clowns. I'm a mess. I think ugly thoughts, fantasize unholy scenarios, whisper nasty words, and need daily showers in the cleansing love of God.

And don't go looking at me with that superior tilt to your head; I am in very good company. Even the great apostle Paul lamented, "The good that I will to do, I do not do; but the evil I will not to do, that I practice" (Romans 7:19).

Translation: If you could look inside me, you'd see an epic mess.

Yes, I clean up nicely. Yes, I can stand and preach the great truths of Scripture, and do it with all sincerity and love. I'm capable of great good—as are you, no doubt.

At the same time, there is a part of me so morally wrecked that no amount of paying forward, giving back, Kingdom building, or neighbor loving will render me fit company for God.

Until I feel that immutable truth deep down in my bones, I will find no amazement in the grace that lifted me out from the miry clay.

That's been my point all along.

Grace is the fearsome force that flows unceasingly from God's heart and bridges the gap between his unscalable heights and my unfathomable depths.

Any vain imagination that would seek to scale down God spoils grace.

Any similar delusion that would minimize my depravity also spoils grace.

The bigger the gap, the more amazing the grace. Don't confuse God with a teddy bear. Grace doesn't make him spineless. He doesn't save everybody. Doesn't wink at sin. Doesn't lower his standards.

The Two Debtors

Jesus told a parable about two debtors who were inches away from getting their kneecaps blasted by their bookie's goons. (Please bear with my loose paraphrase of the story.) Moocher #1 was in for half a mil, and Moocher #2 for fifty grand.

The bookie, feeling especially generous due to a particularly delicious plate of lasagna set before him, rubbed his belly and forgave both moochers.

Which one, Jesus asked, would love the bookie more?

The most interesting factoid about this parable is the setting in which Jesus told it—a party plagued by GDD. The ultra-holy partygoers were scandalized when "a woman in the city who was a sinner" washed Jesus' feet with her tears and anointed them with costly oil (Luke 7:37).

After sucking half the oxygen out of the room, the professional legalists heaped their unspoken judgments on Jesus.

Jesus egged them on, by reading their minds, by telling this parable, and by nailing his sanctimonious host for failing to offer even the most basic of courtesies.

Compared to the sinful woman, the self-proclaimed "holy" host loved Jesus very little.

The upshot of the story is Christ's scathing statement to his host: "Therefore I say to you, her sins, which are many, are forgiven, for she loved much. But to whom little is forgiven, the same loves little" (Luke 7:47).

I imagine Jesus staring his host straight in the eye for that last part. *Yeah, buddy, I'm talking about you.*

Every time we minimize our sins, we minimize our forgiveness.

When we minimize our forgiveness, we minimize God's grace.

When we minimize grace, we transmogrify it from grace into a boring tolerance, fit only for theological slackers who insist everyone should get a trophy.

Until you can look at yourself in the mirror and confess, "I am the chief of sinners" (see 1 Timothy 1:15), grace will never be a big deal to you. And your love for God— regardless of how busy you are for his Kingdom—will be little.

Amazing

That a God who hates sin should love me, knowing my sins, is amazing.

That a God who knows all things and never forgets a subatomic wiggle, should cast my sins behind his back into a sea of forgetfulness, is amazing.

That a person who deserves divine wrath should stand before the cosmic court free from condemnation forever, is amazing.

That a bankrupt sinner should be lavished with the riches of divine grace, is amazing.

That a Savior who was spit upon and rejected by the people he came to save should cry out, "Father, forgive them for they know not what they do," is amazing.

That a conscience loaded with guilt and shame, can be cleansed and re-cleansed over and over and over again, is amazing.

That no sin, no matter how heinous, is beyond the reach

of God's forgiveness through the blood of Calvary's cross, is amazing.

That a repeat offender can receive repeat forgiveness, is amazing.

That a God of infinite perfection can delight in a perpetrator of infinite iniquity, is amazing.

That heaven can be populated by scoundrels like me, is amazing.

That grace is offered freely, paid in full through the blood of the Lamb, to those without anything worth giving in return, is amazing.

That heaven is mine, eternal life is mine, an inheritance is mine, glory is mine, power is mine, peace is mine, salvation is mine, forgiveness is mine, and anything good from God whatsoever—knowing the carnival of craziness lurking beneath my placid pastoral exterior—is mine, is utterly, irretrievably, and eternally amazing.

Back to Grace

Neo-legalism has a fundamental problem: by blurring the distinction between saved and not saved, it douses grace's amazingness in the tepid waters of tolerance.

It invites "belonging before believing," which is fine; but many times it never gets around to *believing*, which is not fine. When people currently known to be lost are invited into full partnership with the people of God, they gain such insider status with God's people that they can easily forget their outsider status with God himself. Their inclusion in the church redefines the church from a mystical fellowship of blood-bought saints into a pragmatic community of good people doing nice things together.

I teach juniors and seniors at a Christian college—Bible, theology, and ministry majors—and still find students who are active in church but "dead in trespasses and sins" (Ephesians 2:1). Several students have reported they were saved in my classes when we covered the Cross and what salvation means.

They had never connected the death of Christ on the cross with their eternal salvation.

These students were preparing to be pastors. Some were about to graduate. They were active in church leadership, but they had never crossed the threshold of faith. They were active in campus ministry, Christian community, and world service. They were busy for Jesus and acting in community with his people, *but they were still in their sins.*

They had mastered the fine art of social acceptance. Some could be described as cool. Hip, even. Respected Christian leaders all. They were included. They belonged.

But they were not born again.

How can this be?

Could it be their peer Christian culture has been infected by Grace Deficit Disorder? God help us if it ever becomes the norm that the decisive moment of salvation evaporates into a fuzzy "doing the Christian thing."

The critical question is not *what have you done with church*, but *what have you done with Christ?*

To imagine that one can gain salvation by conforming to the Christianized social norm is to imply God has lowered his standards.

That is not grace.

Besides, it's impossible. If God lowered his standards, who would ever need the "wideness in God's mercy"?[26] If we've turned his lion's roar into a good buddy's attaboy, and his wrath into a grumpy disposition chased away by the New Testament era, then why did we need a bloodied Savior?

Surprise! The junk in your life is still junky. It never stops being junky. "Belonging" to the Christian tribe doesn't change that fact. Only believing in the Savior does. Belonging doesn't cleanse us from sin. God still wants to yank it out, roots and all. He doesn't love it, doesn't like the smell, and doesn't cancel his agenda that will one day make us clean as fresh-fallen snow (Isaiah 1:18).

Grace is anti-sin. Always will be.

Even if you're busy in the church.

Even if you're helping children.

You, in your sins, are as far from God's saving embrace as the east is from the west, no matter how many Catalyst-Passion-Hillsong-Velocity-Verge-Exponential-Thrive conferences you've been to (no offense intended). You must be born again.

Are You Saved?

A holy God is intolerant. He must be, or he would cease being God. But his radical intolerance becomes your best friend in this sense: *God hates the stuff that breaks your heart.*

He doesn't tolerate it, not even for a nanosecond. His intolerance for that which diminishes you, demeans you, damages you, and damns you knows no bounds. He flexes his muscular arm to yank it out of your life and to crush it like a grape in a winepress. God has declared war against your sin—which required the ultimate aggression waged by the ultimate warrior. Never was divine intolerance for sin put on display as it was at Calvary. To bypass the message of the Cross is to spew Grace Deficit Disorder throughout your soul.

How would you like to live in a universe where God was okay with the slime of sin? No thanks.

God can only tolerate those who are positioned in the shadow of the Cross. And that begins with a definable moment in your life called *getting saved*.

You can serve Jesus and speak Christianese and over time come to assume you have closed the gap between yourself and God. That assumption is wrong. That assumption could have eternal consequences.

I sought God so hard it hurt. I climbed the ladder of performance till my little legs wore out. Reached and strained and stretched and labored to attain to his lofty stature.

In the end, it was almost too good to be true. God closed the gap between himself and me all by his lonesome.

I just said yes to grace; that was enough.

And that simply blows my mind.

CHAPTER 6

WORLDLINESS

You and I have need of the strongest spell that can be found
to wake us from the evil enchantment of worldliness.[27]
C. S. LEWIS

A True Conversation

A youth pastor (YP) who heads a thriving ministry of almost two hundred high school students in an urban setting, the vast majority of whom are from unchurched families, meets with SP, the newly installed senior pastor of the struggling church of about three hundred people.

SP: I want to talk with you about some concerns.

YP: Sure. What's up?

SP: It has come to my attention you're using "Christian rock and roll" [air quotes] in the youth group. Is that right?

YP: [fidgets in chair] Um...yes, sir. Why do you ask?

SP: [looking somber] Some of our parents have told me. And they are very concerned. They are grieved. They don't want their children corrupted with worldly music. [YP does a quick mental calculation: only five families in the church have kids of high school age. He figures out who probably complained.]

YP: [resisting urge to roll eyes] Yes, sir. So...what are you saying?

SP: You can't use Christian rock and roll music anymore in the youth group.

YP: [mental panic] Well, what kind of music can I use? Most of these kids have no church background at all.

SP: You just need to tone it down.

YP: Well, how can I tell when it's actually rock and roll? Where's the line?

SP: You know the song that Sally sang in church last Sunday?

YP: [Nods. It was Sandi Patti's "Via Dolorosa," a gorgeously gut-wrenching 1990s ballad about Jesus' journey to the cross, sung by a soprano, complete with an orchestral-style sound track on cassette tape. YP envisions students with shoulder-length hair and Black Sabbath T-shirts throwing tomatoes.] Yes.

SP: You can't use anything more rocky than that.

YP: [gulps] Yes, sir.

A few weeks later, YP was obliged to sit through a grueling, special "holiness event," with a speaker brought in to teach the church why there is no such thing as Christian rock, and how drums appeal to our sensual side and are, therefore, worldly. But harmony is godly.

And thus, another soaring opportunity to reach vulnerable students for Christ was shot out of the sky by the ubiquitous society of Separated Christians Opposed to Worldly Living (SCOWL).

The charge of "worldliness" is a cudgel that has bludgeoned many happy occasions to an early demise. Wherever true grace raises its hopeful head, SCOWL is there to beat it down. They were there to hurl lightning bolts over the frolicsome barbecue when the prodigal son came home. They vociferously opposed King David's half-naked worship dance when the ark of the Lord was returned to Jerusalem. They even sent envoys to newly planted churches in Asia Minor to correct the excesses of that notorious libertine, Paul.

They created odd substitutes for proms and drove my cousin to paste false labels over her Beatles albums in the 1960s to avoid her Christian boarding school wardens. In more recent days, SCOWL drove young people out of the churches in droves through a season of skirmishes called worship wars.

I cringe to think of all the years I spent in SCOWL as a member in good standing. Thank God for grace.

Worldliness

The writers of Scripture leave no doubt when they address the dangers of worldliness:

1 John 2:15: Do not love the world or the things in the world. If anyone loves the world, the love of the Father is not in him.

Romans 12:2: Do not be conformed to this world, but be transformed by the renewing of your mind, that you may prove what is that good and acceptable and perfect will of God.

James 4:4: *Adulterers and adulteresses! Do you not know that friendship with the world is enmity with God? Whoever therefore wants to be a friend of the world makes himself an enemy of God.*

Loving the world, being conformed to the world, and being a friend of the world are truly out of bounds. This raises some tricky questions: How can we as Christians be *in* the world but not *of* the world? How can we relate to the world around us in non-legalistic ways?

Worldliness, Then and Now

Traditional legalism's approach to worldliness can be summed up in one word: *separation.* Whether from the lips of rock-and-roll-bashing fundamentalists or zipper-prohibiting Amish, the clarion cry of traditional holiness remains: "'Come out from among them, and be ye separate,' saith the Lord, 'and touch not the unclean thing; and I will receive you'" (2 Corinthians 6:17 KJV).

One could not love the world's music, for example, and still love God. You had to choose. You had to choose drumless, beatless, harmonious hymns over the world's sensual ruinations. Extra points for a cappella. Bonus for the handbell choir.

Separation meant exhibiting a distinct and visible difference from cultural norms. Good Christians looked, spoke, dressed, moved, sang, drank, wore their hair, and spent their time differently from their worldly neighbors. They *looked* Christian.

They were "a peculiar people" (1 Peter 2:9 KJV), and proudly so.

Having grown up in this separatist subculture, I may surprise you by confessing certain benefits: mainly, it kept me out of trouble.

Separation's downside, however, was that it also kept me out of a lot of legitimate joy. And this is exactly why so many young people, suckled on the bosom of legalism, become poster children for Christians Gone Wild the day they are released from omnipresent parental restraint.

When I applied to Wheaton College, a bastion of evangelicalism, SCOWL members warned me against the school's "worldliness." I explained that students signed a pledge not to dance or go to movies, and that they took down the tennis court nets on Sunday, lest we violate the [day after the] Sabbath.

That wasn't good enough for SCOWL. The college was too broad-minded, they said, and didn't practice "separation."

One church I attended prohibited people who smoked from becoming official members. In its membership brochure, the leaders wrote, "Even though smoking isn't prohibited in the Bible, we feel justified in creating new rules, as long as they are more restrictive than the Bible's."

Indeed.

Perhaps they should have pondered Christ's words: "All too well you reject the commandment of God, that you may keep your tradition" (Mark 7:9).

Later, we discovered that some of those same leaders had created family "hot zones" of pornography or emotional abuse. But thank God they didn't smoke.

The Consequence

Traditional legalists avoided secular institutions like a vegan avoids a pig on a spit. They pulled out of education, entertainment, arts, news, politics, the military, publishing, and economics.

Richard Niebuhr's classic work, *Christ and Culture*, calls this position "Christ against culture." Under this view, Christ squared off in a cage match versus culture, with little hope of reconciliation.[28] After a few pokes in the eye, these "anti-cultural" Christians retreated to their corner and never emerged, choosing to take the difficult path of nonconformity—separating from worldly pleasures and toe-tapping with the Gaithers instead. (No slight to the Gaithers intended: I have all their albums.)

As a consequence of a "Christ against culture" posture, Christians evacuated most societal institutions. This created a Christian-free playground, which we feel today every time we complain about how the media portray Christians as horse-and-buggy-riding terrorists-in-the-making. Could it be that the anti-Christian propaganda, the anything-goes sexuality in entertainment, and the culture of cruelty defined by middle-school mean girls are, in part, the rancid fruit of Christians having left the world's institutions?

When the Christians escaped, where did they go?

They created a parallel universe: Christian media, Christian education, Christian arts, Christian entertainment, and Christian publishing.

But let's not wag the shame finger too vigorously at our escapist friends. In many cases, they were shoved to the side unwillingly. For example, there's hardly a secular publisher that would touch a book with an overtly Christian theme today. Christians face an increasingly difficult dilemma: as aspects of our culture swirl down the moral drain, we can either hop in, valiantly trying to plug the whole, or stand on the rim, rendering ourselves ever more marginalized.

A lot like Daniel in Babylon.

Or Paul in Ephesus or Rome.

Escapist approaches to worldliness can still work some magic. I don't want my kids learning sex education with a group of horny middle-schoolers from a teacher whose value system starts with the survival of the fittest. We've opted out of that stuff for good reason.

While there's a logic to the Christ-against-culture mindset, there's a danger to it as well. Jesus declared us "salt of the earth"; we can't remove society's only preservative without expecting the meat to rot.

So along came neo-legalism to shove the pendulum too far the other way.

Neo-Worldliness

Neo-legalism serves up neo-worldliness in three flavors:

1. Embracing culture indiscriminately

From full-sleeve tattoos to abundant piercings to rabbinical facial hair, it's Christian-hip to be culturally relevant. Perhaps in reaction to excessive cultural separatism, today's Christians get down and dirty with the prevailing culture. We're advised to look, sound, act, eat, and smell like our spiritually lost peers.

There is true value in this position. Thank God for Christ-followers willing to speak the language of the streets. Paul said, "I have become all things to all men, that I might by all means save some" (1 Corinthians 9:22). That's not worldliness; that's just love.

Whereas traditional legalists withdrew from culture, it is quite possible neo-legalists have embraced it too tightly.

An evangelical church offered a Christmas dance at a swanky hotel, complete with an open bar serving hard liquor. "I'll have a Dewar's on the rocks please, and 'Deck the Halls' in Jesus' name."

Another church I know of conducted a Vegas Night fundraiser in their fellowship hall. Still barely recovering from my own traditional legalism, I ventured a peek, just to see. (Okay, I wanted to judge them.) Roulette tables, card tables, and craps tables littered the smoke-filled room. A bank of slot machines added to the clamor. To cap it off, cocktail waitresses wearing Playboy Bunny outfits delivered hard liquor to happy worshippers—er, patrons. Fellowship indeed.

Would it be legalistic of me to be mortified by that?

Worldliness, as I'm going to suggest, is a heart problem, above all else. It is a symptom of Grace Deficit Disorder, in which the sense of deficit drives a person to cling to inferior sources of joy at the expense of embracing God.

Call me un-hip, but a church offering Playboy Bunnies might be filling that deficit the wrong way. God never calls his people to demean people in order to reach people.

2. Preaching the gospel in actions, but not words

A deeper worldliness than embracing some of culture's decadent forms affects neo-legalism and infects whole swaths of Christendom. It is found in the groundswell of neo-voices who suggest that acts of mercy and compassion done in Christ's name are enough to communicate the gospel. A pastor who ministered to the poorest of the poor in one of Chicago's toughest neighborhoods told me that hugging a child was giving the child the gospel.

Niebuhr might have called this view "Christ the Transformer of Culture."[29] Its practitioners roll up their sleeves and get their hands dirty for the betterment of the world by the sweat of their brow.

A century ago, Walter Rauschenbusch, the father of what came to be called the social gospel, declared, "It is not a matter of getting individuals into heaven, but of transforming the life on earth into the harmony of heaven."[30]

Later theologians picked up this football and ran with it, all the way to the end zone of a Christless gospel: love is all that matters.

But do social ministry and proclamation of the gospel have to be an either/or proposition? Shouldn't they walk hand in hand? Shouldn't Christians be about both getting individuals into heaven *and* transforming the life on earth?

One missionary surgeon, notable for building hospitals in Africa and training surgeons for ministry in emerging nations, said, "What good is it if we heal their bodies, but ultimately their souls go to hell?"[31]

Though working for good in society is essential, it is not the whole gospel. Alleviating suffering in the world expresses the gospel, in a way. It serves the gospel by opening doors and lending credibility to our words. But the gospel is first and foremost the announcement of a Savior who delivers from sin and its eternal consequences. All the other good stuff—important as it is—remains a by-product of the gospel.

Saint Francis's famous dictum may have started the whole ball rolling: "Preach the gospel at all times; if necessary, use words."

One observer replies, "Saying, 'Preach the gospel; if necessary use words,' is like saying, 'Tell me your phone number; if necessary, use digits.' "[32]

"How shall they believe in Him of whom they have not heard?" (Romans 10:14).

Like the Ethiopian official met by Philip, the human cry remains, "How can I [understand], unless someone guides me?" (Acts 8:31).

Among neo-legalists, a variation on the social gospel theme can include political activism. In a free society, it is crucial for Christ's people to speak Christ's truth into the political realm. It is essential to incarnate Christ's presence within the halls of power. Even so, does it not constitute worldliness to pin our hopes to a political process? When the first generation of disciples "turned the world upside down," they did it largely without maneuvering the levers of earthly power.

We could fix every broken system of human government, and people still wouldn't be saved. That's not where our hopes lie.

When neo-worldliness defines the gospel in terms of doing good in this world only—to the exclusion of eternal salvation from the consequences of sin—it swallows the fatal pill that ends the gospel at a person's death.

Then what happens? How have we have alleviated suffering in the world to come?

I'm a strong advocate for both social ministry and old-fashioned evangelism. Both. Not either/or. But this I know: if we don't make heaven big, we can't make earth right.

The conversionist approach sounds great in theory. The practice, however, gets dicey. That's because, too many times, the only person transformed is the Christian, who set out to change the world, but winds up being crushed into the world's ungodly shape.

Two millennia ago, Paul advised, "Don't let the world around you squeeze you into its own mould" (Romans 12:2 PHILLIPS). Christians ever since have engaged a tricky dance with the world and its prickly systems, delivering saving grace and redemptive love while trying to avoid the contagion of worldliness.

3. Chasing an experience

I admire any generation of Christ followers devoted to moving their faith from head to heart. To many younger Christ followers, the intellectualized God of traditional legalism looks like a giant ugly brain on a pedestal. Where's the love? Where's the heart? Where's the compassion? Where's the experience?

A faith that isn't self-authenticating won't make the cut.

But that raises a big question: *How does faith prove itself?*

The answer, for many neo-legalists, is simple: through a direct encounter with God. I *feel* God, *hear* God, *touch* God, and *sway in the presence* of God. Many will flock to conferences, rock concerts, bars, or any experience—the more intense the better—that will pierce life's boredom enough to grant the slightest flash of transcendence.

"Touch me, God," is the prayer.

The legalism here is subtle.

The pursuit of a tangible encounter with God risks making the voice of experience louder than the voice of God in Scripture. This sets up the same error the Pharisees fell into: self-made traditions wash like a tsunami over Scripture. Paradosis trumps the Word. Self-interpreted, self-defined, self-created experiential moments end up having more truth-authority than God who has spoken decisively and finally in his Word.

Who, then, occupies the heart's throne?

Self.

One lesson I've learned the hard way: *self* is a lousy ruler.

Thomas encountered the risen Savior and believed. Jesus was okay with that, but not totally. "Thomas, because you have seen Me, you have believed. Blessed are those who have not seen and yet have believed" (John 20:29).

There's just something about naked faith trusting in naked grace (offered by simple Scriptures) that makes God happy. Feeling or no feeling. Encounter or no encounter. Faith is the victory that overcomes the world (1 John 5:4).

What Is Worldliness?

Worldliness is first and foremost a philosophy, over against a set of actions. It provides a Theory of Everything for those who prefer not to submit to God. This philosophy stretches its tentacles into every major institution of culture: art, entertainment, education, government, philosophy, industry, and religion.

The Greek word *kosmos* can refer to the earth, the people on earth, or nature's beauty on earth. Perhaps more relevant, it can also mean "the whole circle of earthly goods, endowments, riches, advantages, pleasures, etc., which although hollow and frail and fleeting, stir desire, seduce from God, and are obstacles to the cause of Christ."[33] In this sense, the kosmos is a world system that has gone sideways with God.

Worldliness ferments together three toxic ingredients: independence from God, seduction from reality, and forgetfulness of eternity, all of which come packaged in the form of subtle lies called "doctrines of demons" (1 Timothy 4:1).

It's easiest to understand worldliness as the philosophy of a happy life cooked up by Satan in his continuing efforts to displace God. "The whole world [kosmos, world system] lies under the sway of the wicked one" (1 John 5:19), writes the apostle John. Jesus called Satan "the ruler of this world [kosmos]" (John 12:31), and Paul called him "the god of this age" (2 Corinthians 4:4).

The founder of Dallas Theological Seminary, Lewis Sperry Chafer, called it the "*cosmos diabolicus*," the devil's world—a clear Christ-against-culture statement.[34]

In this view, Satan attacks people through a seductive world system that cooks up a toxic faith in a toxic god with a toxic lifestyle, slathered in delicious humanistic frosting.

Whether or not you dance, drink, watch movies, or groove to cool rhythms, if you adopt a philosophy of independence from God, you are worldly. You can thumb your nose at God even as you seek social justice, or alleviate the world's sufferings, or evangelize lost people.

The world isn't the problem.

Worldliness is.

A Gracified View of Worldliness

Grace invites you to look to God for your joy, support, satisfaction, and purpose. Not only is he your central source of these things, he is also your best friend. This is all-important. Notice the core of James's blast against of worldliness:

> *Adulterers and adulteresses! Do you not know that friendship with the world is enmity [hostility] with God? Whoever therefore wants to be a friend of the world makes himself an enemy of God. (James 4:4)*

Worldliness is, at its core, a symptom of Grace Deficit Disorder. You surmise that God and his grace are insufficient for you, so you turn elsewhere. Worldliness is a relational malfunction in which you find your deepest emotional satisfaction in inferior sources, at the expense of your relationship with God. Hence, James's use of the labels "adulterers" and "adulteresses."

Friendship with the world system and friendship with God are mutually exclusive: you can only choose one. It's like having two milkshakes and only one straw. You can't suck on the strawberry shake and the chocolate shake at the same time. You have to choose.

And you can't draw your life's deepest fulfillment from God and this devil-infused world system at the same time, either.

What you have with God is a relationship.

What you have with the world system is also a relationship—only in this relationship, your partner is desperately trying to cut God out of the picture. See how they can't go together?

Gracification is a way of life in which you constantly turn to God in faith and expectation, resting in his promises, trusting his omnipotence, and delighting in his providence. A gracified life is a satisfied life, a happy life, a life that smiles at the world's allurements and says *no thanks—I'm doing fine without you.*

A Person

We haven't nearly exhausted the ways in which Christians put together Christ and culture, but let's jump to the bottom line. How can Christians avoid the bear traps of worldliness without getting tangled in the snares of legalism?

Jesus said, "Come to Me" (Matthew 11:28). To me, the person.

He lamented over legalists who were "not willing to come to Me that [they] may have life" (John 5:40). They had come to a philosophy, or to a religious system, but they had never come to him as a person.

He told his disciples, "Let the little children come to Me" (Mark 10:14).

And he invited anyone who was spiritually thirsty to "come

to Me" (John 7:37).

All the doctrinal, theological, and factual realities of Christianity add up to this mother of all truths: in Jesus, life with God is a person-to-person communion.

When we're more attached to our philosophies than to Jesus, we've been hypnotized by the devil's kosmos, even if that philosophy does great things in this world or the next. Even if that philosophy offers intense emotional experiences.

"Wasn't that awesome?" needs to become "Isn't Jesus awesome!"

Wake up and come to Jesus.

Know him. Hear him. Appreciate him. Receive from him. Sit at his feet and learn of him. Rest in his love. Sink deep roots into his grace. Have a heart for lost people, and don't be surprised at the mess they're in. Remember where you came from; embracing lost people doesn't make you worldly (1 Corinthians 5:9–10).

Being against bad stuff doesn't deliver us from worldliness. It's being *for* Jesus Christ that does the trick. Paul declared himself "separated to the gospel of God," and from that separation flowed life-giving fountains of grace still working their magic today.

Bind your heart to God and his gospel and, whether your thing is world service, tattooed arms, pierced body parts, urban living, disco dancing, responsible adult drinking—or conservative values, Gaither homecomings, crew cuts, skorts, and total abstinence—it won't make a bit of difference, because you will have overcome the Grace Deficit Disorder that makes worldliness so devastating.

Bind your heart to God and follow his call on your life, no

matter what the members of SCOWL say.

If God calls you to monastic seclusion, then wear out your knees on rough stone floors, fervent in prevailing prayer.

If he calls you to reach wealthy people for Jesus, then share Christ faithfully to earth's Donald Trumps.

If he calls you to witness to a friend over hot wings and beer, then go for a local brew.

If he calls you to total abstinence and a cappella harmonies, then stay pure and sing your lungs out in the church choir, but don't forget lost people.

If he calls you to another day of pressing through a boatload of adversities, grateful to have just survived, then thank him for his grace, and speak an encouraging word along the way.

If he calls you to disciple future pastors poolside amidst the aroma of fine cigars, then puff with gusto. When a SCOWL operative chastised the great Charles H. Spurgeon for smoking cigars, he answered that it would only be sinful to smoke them to excess. Legend has it, when asked to define excess, Spurgeon answered, "Smoking two cigars at once."

You go, Chuck.

Whatever God may call you to, follow him and allow for the fact that his call on the next person's life may look radically different from his call on yours.

If God has your heart, then the devil's world doesn't. Grace wins. However else you might roll together Christ and culture, at this point, it no longer matters. I have to believe there's enough wideness in God's mercy to embrace a whole lot of differing opinions on worldly behaviors as long as he truly, deeply has your heart.

CHAPTER 7

SHALLOW

Ignorance of Scripture is ignorance of Christ.
JEROME (300s)

Confidence that one's impressions are God-given
is no guarantee that this is really so, even when they
persist and grow stronger through long seasons of
prayer. Bible-based wisdom must judge them.
J. I. PACKER (1900s)

In 1983, the J. Paul Getty Museum acquired a statue called a *kouros*—what appeared to be an exquisite 2,500-year-old Greek marble sculpture of a naked boy. What distinguished the Getty kouros from others of its type was its condition: one of the most flawless and intact ever discovered, certainly worth the $10 million price tag.

Until questions over its authenticity began to fly.

In his 2005 bestseller, *Blink*, Malcolm Gladwell describes how the museum showed the statue to several renowned experts, who soon became part of a growing chorus of naysayers.[35]

To one expert, the fingernails seemed wrong. Another observer, a former director of the Metropolitan Museum of Art, said the statue looked too "fresh" be authentic.

When sculpture and antiquities expert Evelyn Harrison heard of the museum's commitment to purchase the kouros, she took one look at the statue and said, "I'm sorry to hear that."[36]

Yet another expert, Angelos Delivorrias, "felt a wave of intuitive repulsion" as soon as he laid eyes on the kouros.[37]

Gladwell describes others who also felt that something was awry. Many formed this judgment in the blink of an eye; they couldn't even say why.

How did they know?

Decades of dedicated study and experience had stocked their mental databases with libraries of data. When they saw the kouros, their brains compiled the visual data before them, compared it to mountains of stored facts, concluded something was wrong, and tied their guts in a knot over the barely perceptible discrepancies.

All this happened in a flash—so fast their conscious thoughts couldn't keep up.

These experts just knew. They experienced what Gladwell calls "the power of thinking without thinking," or what generations of sages have called wisdom.

Wisdom

Wisdom will enter your heart, and knowledge will fill you with joy. Wise choices will watch over you. Understanding will keep you safe. Wisdom will save you from evil people, from those whose words are twisted. (Proverbs 2:10–12 NLT)

Wisdom might also save you from buying a counterfeit statue. For the Christian, wisdom is biblical knowledge on steroids. It is the knowledge of God's deep truths, not as sequins bedazzled onto blue jeans, but as the very warp and woof of the fabric. Wisdom is God's truth integrated so deeply into the soul, that the wise can smell a lie before they can even explain it: Their senses have been "exercised to discern both good and evil" (Hebrews 5:14 KJV).

Do you remember being taught to go with your first instinct when taking a test? Your teachers were right, but only if you had studied. Your gut would tell you the right answer before your brain could figure it out. In reality, your brain *had* figured it out, because you were a great student and had prepared for the test, but your gut just knew it first.

Without studying, however, following your gut would net you a score only as good as a chimpanzee taking the same test. Like my wife's college students that dreadful day.

Your gut needs training or you can't trust it—you can only be "wise in [your] own eyes," a decidedly foolish position (Proverbs 26:12) and a sure symptom of Grace Deficit Disorder.

When you have wisdom, you know God as he wants you to know him. When you have wisdom, you've tuned your heart to the same harmonic frequency as Christ tuned his. Wisdom puts you in possession of the very laws that govern life, love, and the whole created order. Wisdom installs the law of grace, the grace operating system, into your soul.

"Wisdom is the principal thing; therefore get wisdom" (Proverbs 4:7).

Legalism thumbs its nose at wisdom in one of two ways.

Traditional legalists bypass the soul of wisdom, accepting the letter of truth, but not the spirit. That's why traditional legalists can spout orthodox theology on Sunday morning while treating their spouses like dirt on Sunday afternoon. Academic knowledge does not equate to gracified living.

Neo-legalists delude themselves by thinking they can have the spirit of divine truth without the letter of truth. "It's not about theology," they say. "It's just about love/Jesus/world peace/doing good." A resulting lack of wisdom makes them suckers for manipulation. It also dooms them to rapid burnout. Activist knowledge falls short of gracified living, too.

Anti-wisdom clichés sprout like weeds: "Christians don't need to *know* more; they need to *do* more," and "Most Christians are educated beyond their obedience," and "Jesus is not going to say 'well thought, good and faithful servant'; he's going to say 'well done.'"

The simple truth of Christian service is that you can never hear "well done" unless your Christian life was well thought. The teaching ministry of the church is not optional. The first half of each epistle teaches "well thought." The second half teaches "well done" and is utterly dependent on the first. Only a fool would skip the dance lessons and expect to look good on the ballroom dance floor.

Even so, both academic knowledge alone (traditional legalism) and activist practice alone (neo-legalism) fall short of wisdom's lofty standards.

In either case, true wisdom gets kicked to the curb, and with it, the ability to discern good from evil, truth from error, orthodoxy from heterodoxy, love from manipulation, and character from charisma.

A Mile Wide and an Inch Deep

Dorothy Sayers warned our grandparents, "It is worse than useless for Christians to talk about the importance of Christian morality, unless they are prepared to take their stand upon the fundamentals of Christian theology."[38]

Worse than useless? Why?

Because the grace operating system is an integrated structure of interlocking truths, such that every other doctrine of ministry and life depends on it. Grace is not something you can hear about once or twice and think you're done. Writing its code into your life calls for long-term study, diligence, intensity, faith, and humility—an extreme devotion to enter into the heart of God.

Wisdom and Grace

Grace in life—gracification—requires taking our stand on the "fundamentals of Christian theology," to quote Sayers.

Without such heart-renewal, Christian morality begins its inexorable descent into legalism.

Platitudes from misinformed preachers about too much Bible and not enough obedience only discourage the half-starved people of God from feasting on the meat of the Word. Pastors, directed by Christ himself to feed the flock, morph into Pharaoh's taskmasters, flogging God's people to make bricks for the pastors' edifices, while neglecting the one food that can make them strong.

The founder of Dallas Theological Seminary begins his book on grace with these immortal words: "The precise and discriminate meaning of the word *grace* should be crystal clear to every child of God."[39]

Amen.

How shall they come to this clarity without Scripture?

And how shall they engage Scripture unless they be taught?

And how shall they be taught unless preachers roll up their sleeves and follow the apostolic marching orders: "We will give ourselves continually to prayer and to the ministry of the word" (Acts 6:4)?

What is grace? Grace is a force in God's heart, a policy in God's plan, and a gift of God's love. We don't deserve it. We'll never earn it. And we can't pay it back.

People think that *grace* means God is nice; but it doesn't, because he isn't, at least not always. He is inflexibly just, thus making the universe tolerable and giving hope for a future world. In a beautiful twist we humans never saw coming, God satisfied his own strict justice by his Son's great sacrifice. By the Cross, God can bless my putrid soul without defiling his perfect holiness.

There was a day when I stepped into this grace by receiving

Jesus as my Savior—through faith alone in Christ alone. The free gift of eternal life was mine. The assurance of eternal security was mine. And the daily presence of God was also mine. When I look inside myself and see the ugliness there, I can only say: "Amazing grace, how sweet the sound that saved a wretch like me."

That is my testimony.

But it is a testimony rooted in a deep theology.

A shallow view of grace morphs grace into leniency.

A shallow view of grace pares the claws of the Lion of the tribe of Judah.

A shallow view of grace makes God into a wimp.

A shallow view of grace offers a conditional forgiveness and a duty-based holiness.

A shallow view of grace empties hell, robbing the cosmos of final justice.

A shallow view of grace turns a cold shoulder to theology, even as it dances with the wolves of emotionalism and subjectivism.

A shallow view of grace casts a suspicious eye at God's tough love, demotes divine Providence into a romp through a health-and-wealth wonderland, and finds truth in emotion and experience with only passing reference to the written revelation of God.

To swim in the shallow end of theology's pool is to rob grace of its wonder. It is to transform the unparalleled characteristic of the entire Christian revelation claim into a bland generality shared by any religion with the slightest concern for the world's abandoned puppies.

Back to Theology

I am arguing for a wholesale scramble back to theology—for unabashed theological preaching from the pulpits of the land. For Christian education that educates. Give us a Spurgeon, a Lloyd-Jones, a Barnhouse. Restore the likes of William R. Newell, and S. Lewis Johnson. Amy Carmichael preached in India and never strayed from "Calvary love." Henrietta Mears taught the Bible systematically, and out came Bill Bright and Billy Graham. Give us pulpit giants and Bible class teachers who dig deep wells into the springs of truth.

May God give us truth on fire from the pulpits of this land, marinated in rigorous studies, saturated with mercy and grace, igniting revival in the hearts of God's people.

No, I'm not denying the need for "practical" preaching. But practical preaching alone almost always becomes legalistic. That's because the moment a preacher decouples the practices of the Christian life from the theological structures that both *empower* them and *require* them, the poor Christian is left with nothing but a "grunt it out" Christianity. If I can tell a group of people how to live their lives divorced from the grace-infused wisdom of God, then how am I different from Oprah? Or from any other motivational speaker?

Besides, what if the most significant "practical application" of a sermon is simply the internal rewiring of a reverse-polarized soul? Isn't it practical to create interlocked systems of truth in a hearer's soul? Isn't that the only way a hearer becomes a doer? Isn't it practical to demolish lies? Isn't it practical to correct a hearer's sense of identity? Isn't it practical to comfort the afflicted, even if they don't go forth and do anything? Isn't it practical to know the attributes, character, names, and ways of God? Isn't it practical to know God as a Trinity?

Daniel said, "The people who know their God shall be strong, and carry out great exploits" (Daniel 11:32).

Jesus prayed, "Sanctify them by Your truth. Your word is truth" (John 17:17).

Theology is practical. When Christ's flock takes in the Word of God, they don't just get information, they also get power (Hebrews 4:12). Scripture brings divine power into the soul, and creates a supernatural edifice of faith. Like radio-active pellets, every promise, every doctrine, every scriptural principle and truth, emanates the power of God. It displaces human imaginations. It washes out a lifetime of crud. It installs God's own power, God's own grace, to do by his strength what we could never do on our own.

Our people rub shoulders with sophisticated pagans every day. Don't they need buttressing from the devil's lies and answers to the skeptic's questions?

Truth is reality. Anchoring Christians in truth is the foundational function of the church. Everything else flows out of this.

Enough with self-help; it's God's help we need.

Enough with religious activism anchored in emotion; it's true evangelism we need, catalyzed by God's truth, with God's power, for the sake of God's lost sheep.

Enough boasting over what our churches are doing for God; let him who boasts, boast in Jesus Christ and in him crucified. I tell my church frequently that I don't feel good when people say, "What a great sermon!" or "What a great church!" I want them to say, "What a great God!" and "What a great mission we're on: helping people to find and follow God."

Dumbed-Down Christianity

Mark Noll jabbed the church in the eye when he wrote, "The scandal of the evangelical mind is that there is not much of an evangelical mind."[40]

Can't anything be done about epidemic levels of biblical illiteracy? Don't we care? Where's the mad scramble to heal this gaping wound in the body of Christ?

It is a sad mistake to say most Christians are educated beyond their obedience. Studies show most aren't educated at all.[41] The crisis of ignorance in the body of Christ is a reflection of Grace Deficit Disorder, by which the preaching of shoulds and shouldn'ts has all but displaced the preaching of who God is, what he has decisively done through Christ, and what he stands to do for and in the believer.

Researcher David Kinnaman says:

> *Most Americans do not have strong and clear beliefs, largely because they do not possess a coherent biblical worldview. . . . That is, they lack a consistent and holistic understanding of their faith. Millions of Americans say they are personally committed to Jesus Christ, but they believe he sinned while on earth. Many believers claim to trust what the Bible teaches, but they reject the notion of a real spiritual adversary or they feel that faith-sharing activities are optional.*

*Millions feel personally committed to God, but they
are renegotiating the definition of that deity.*[42]

Dorothy Sayers lamented, "The brutal fact is that in this Christian country not one person in a hundred has the faintest notion of what the Church teaches about God or man or society or the person of Jesus Christ."[43] It is as true today as it was in her World War II generation.

Traditional legalism substitutes cookbook rules for true wisdom. Neo-legalism prefers world-changing activity to wisdom, pressuring Marys to be Marthas.

The simple truth will never go away: you can't live like Christ unless you think like Christ; and you can't think like Christ without knowing the Bible.

Grace rises up within the heart as a complex structure of truth upon truth. Promises flowing within the Trinity overflow into the household of faith. Divine realities arise from the Cross to cleanse the soul and heal the heart. Grace reaches out to define you. Grace unveils the real you, celebrates your true identity, and empowers you to be your best self.

More complex than a Legoland structure, yet more beautiful than a glorious sunset, the doctrine of grace stands forever as the most exacting, brilliant, coherent truth claim ever revealed to the human heart.

"It is good that the heart be established by grace," says Hebrews 13:9. Let the construction commence.

Dear pastor and church leader, never let a syllable cross your lips that in any way diminishes a person's devotion to the Word of God.

Thank God for a new breed of pastor and church leader

who take their Bible-teaching ministry seriously.

I have no doubt that some reading these words will accuse me of wanting to let the church's social ministry wither on the vine. No, let it thrive by the power of God. But if those engaged in social ministry can articulate neither the theological reasons for doing it, nor the divine power fueling it, nor the evangelistic mandate motivating it, maybe we've got the wrong people on the job.

Grace needs theology—a laser-beam focus on God in his fullness. When the biblical story devolves into an endless succession of self-help hints and evil-whitewashing crusades, God gets relegated to a subplot, and humans become stars in their own tragic comedy. Having dismissed theological depth to the realm of picky seminary professors, the church's puppet masters can yank the church's behavioral strings with impunity. In the name of love. Or refugees. Or any other cause *du jour*.

Any old religion can come up with a moral system. Any religion can create rituals and rules. Any religion can burden mankind with laws, sacrifices, duties, and obligations. Any old religion can jab at the wounds of GDD.

Only the Father of our Lord Jesus Christ offers a beautiful, interlocking truth system of profound grace, highlighting forever what God does for us instead of what we do for him. Grace is the ultimate apologetic; it sets Christianity in a class by itself. No religion has ever come close.

For the church not to understand grace—for the church to dumb it down, for the church to pollute its crystal-clear streams with the murky toxins of legalism—is both the greatest scandal and the greatest tragedy the cause of Christ on earth can endure.

Dorothy Sayers continued:

> *It is a lie to say that dogma [doctrine, theology]*
> *does not matter; it matters enormously. It is fatal*
> *to let people suppose that Christianity is only a*
> *mode of feeling; it is vitally necessary to insist*
> *that it is first and foremost a rational explanation*
> *of the universe. . . . [A] hard, tough, exacting,*
> *and complex doctrine, steeped in a drastic and*
> *uncompromising realism.*[44]

No, doctrine isn't the finish line, but if you don't know the doctrines of grace, you haven't even reached the starting line.

Like the J. Paul Getty kouros (allegedly), how many millions of dollars in the church are going toward counterfeits, all because God's people have been instructed lightly?

Untaught Christians are easy prey for legalists. A wise soul senses seducers, manipulators, abusers, and control freaks a mile away. They just know. Not because they have a "word of knowledge," but because they have the Word of ultimate knowledge, hidden in their hearts, energized by the Holy Spirit. A hardwired, fully installed, grace operating system running in the background all the time produces abundant joy, and grace, and peace, and everything a normal person could ever desire.

Paul prayed, "That I might know him."

God help us to say the same.

CHAPTER 8

FUEL

That the Holy Spirit is the producer in the human heart
of everything that God calls religion, is beyond question
to anyone who accepts Bible statements as divinely true.
He begins, carries on, and consummates in us all spiritual
feeling, all spiritual worship, all spiritual life and energy.
Nor can there be anything more hollow and unreal
than religion without the Holy Spirit.
HORATIO BONAR (1800s)

When I became a youth pastor at the age of twenty, somebody
made a colossal mistake and appointed me to a church board
along with eighteen or so gray-haired gentlemen. Together,
we had the responsibility to guide our congregation into not
being a waste of ecclesiology. As a rookie, I often wondered
what I was doing there, surrounded by leaders of such stature.

At one particularly difficult meeting, we discussed how to
rally more volunteers to staff our ministries.

I asked a dumb question: "So why should anybody in our
church serve God anyway?" I figured if we understood the

motives, we could do a better job encouraging people into ministry.

By the awkward silence that settled over the room, you would have thought I'd just let out a world-class belch.

Grown men fidgeted. One studied his fingernails. A few grunted. We were between senior pastors at the moment, and no one had a ready answer.

Finally, the chairman of our church board, a pillar of faith with pure white hair combed back into a polished helmet, cleared his throat halfway, and looked at me like I was the dumbest piece of meat this side of Chicago's slaughterhouses.

He said, "Because it's their duty."

And that settled that. The meeting moved on.

But I couldn't move on. I was stuck. A thought kept pecking at my spirit like a hungry bird: *Whatever happened to loving God because he first loved us?*

I understood the generational differences here. Our chairman's generation was the "great generation." They sucked it up and got the job done. They defeated Nazism and made the world safe for democracy. I'm grateful. They did their duty without whining, and when they were done, those who survived went back to work with hardly a peep. I thank God for them.

By contrast, my peers and I were young punks, the leading edge of the "entitled generation." Our grandparents did what they did out of duty; we needed a payoff. I get that.

Even so, duty only gets you so far—especially when there's no government-backed draft providing irresistible motivation.

What exactly fuels the church's mission on planet Earth?

Traditional Fuel

Traditional legalism fuels the church's mission through a pipeline of duty, pushed along by guilt and shame. Whatever you're supposed to do, do it because it's right.

Do it because God commanded you.

Do it because you'll feel guilty if you don't.

Do it because bad things will happen—to you, your neighbor, or lost people—if you don't.

Imagine getting flogged—er, motivated—by this hypothetical a few dozen times in your formative years: If you saw your neighbor's house on fire, flames licking through the roof, and you knew your neighbors were asleep on their beds, wouldn't you go crazy banging on the doors trying to rouse them? Wouldn't you do anything—even kick down their front door—to warn them of fiery doom?

If you would do that for a temporal fire, how much more for eternal fires? It's your duty. Anyone with half a heart couldn't pass by without bending every effort to rescue the perishing from eternal perdition.

That house-on-fire illustration owned my tender conscience during my teens and twenties.

Who can argue with hell as a motivation?

In my doctoral program, I wrote an extensive paper on the doctrine of hell as an incentive for evangelism. I argued that everyone with even an ounce of human compassion should feel a duty to contribute their lives to the mission of helping lost people find and follow God. I still feel that way.

It's scriptural. Even the champion of grace, the apostle Paul, writes, "Knowing, therefore, the terror of the Lord, we persuade men" (2 Corinthians 5:11).

The terror of the Lord. Makes you sit up straight just thinking about it.

But there are tremendous differences between a house on fire and hellfire. One is self-evident; the other requires faith. One demands immediate action; the other can wait—at least it feels that way. Rescuing a neighbor from a house fire makes you a hero. Waking a neighbor in the middle of the night to warn of hellfire makes you a lunatic. One merits a medal from a grateful mayor; the other earns you an order of protection from a hacked-off judge.

At times, the traditional legalist's motivation isn't all that motivating.

Neo-Fuel

"A stampede is an act of mass impulse among herd animals or a crowd of people in which the herd (or crowd) collectively begins running with no clear direction or purpose."[45] In a stampede, individuals act without much rational thought. Fueled by adrenaline and fear, they stampede across the horizon, and in a flash they're done.

The third person of the Trinity is God the Holy Spirit. Not God the Holy Adrenaline. Not God the Holy Emotion. Appeals to the emotions have their place, but unless they're backed up by continual and patient instruction in the doctrines and promises of God, they'll fizzle out as fast as open soda on a hot summer day.

In the spiritual realm, passion only goes so far.

That's because we're not designed to run on emotion—not long term at least. Yes, you can sprint to the short-term mission field, spend a weekend raking a neighbor's leaves, and make a difference for God that way. But your motivation won't last. In the marathon of Christian living, you'll soon be grabbing your side and gasping for air.

Emotion flames out too fast. Like a campfire built of straw, it can't last.

But when your passion arises from abiding truths anchored deep within your soul—when the biblical account of your Savior's death gets you choked up—that's when you've got some staying power. Even when God doesn't answer your prayers, even when you feel mad at him, even when you feel he's let you down, you will still serve him. You're acting out of deeply rooted principles, abiding and strong, not out of some preacher's charisma-driven hype.

Gracified wisdom cannot be stampeded.

So yeah, serve God when you're excited.

But when you're not excited, serve him anyway.

Because it's not duty, it's not passion, it's not pity, it's not peer pressure, and it's not fear that fills your gas tank.

It's grace.

Why Serve God?

In *Evangelism in the Early Church*, Michael Green put under a microscope the first generation of Christians after the apostles.[46] He identified three counterintuitive motives that drove the earliest Christians to turn their world upside down. Persecutors hounded these Christians. Paganism and hedonism dominated their cultural worldviews. It was not easy being Christian in the early days. Even so, local groupings of Christ followers served their Savior with unparalleled courage and effect.

Why?

Why did they serve God?

Let's compare Michael Green's discoveries with my church board member's simplistic "because it's their duty."

1. A Sense of Gratitude

You might not realize what a religious explosion the Bible detonated by saying, "God is love" (1 John 4:8, 16). The earliest Christians had grown up with self-serving gods—too many to count. Their high-demand religions traded sacrifice for benefit, an endless *quid pro quo* between humans and the gods. Along came the proclamation of a God of infinite love, a forgiveness of infinite depth, and a heaven of infinite duration—all given freely because of Calvary's love—and men and women gladly stepped forward to carry this gospel to the ends of the known world. Why?

Green writes,

Reflection upon the cross as the supreme impulse to costly service for others in the name of the gospel was unquestionably the greatest single element in keeping the zeal of Christians at fever pitch.[47]

Translation: they served God out of gratitude for the Cross more than out of duty. Green continues, "One finds this same love [of Christ] as the mainspring for Christian service throughout the writings of the second century."[48]

Are you thankful for what God as done for you in Christ? Deeply, humbly thankful? Then serve him.

Perhaps Christians who aren't all that thankful should keep their mouths shut about knowing Jesus. It might be better for them to engage their minds and hearts in the wonders of the Cross. If that doesn't fix their ingratitude, they should seek help.

God has designed the church to serve him out of thankfulness. The same apostle who said, "Knowing, therefore, the terror of the Lord, we persuade men" (2 Corinthians 5:11), quickly added, "For the love of Christ compels us" (2 Corinthians 5:14).

I wish I'd had the guts at that board meeting decades ago to pipe up and say, "If all you've got is duty without gratitude, then maybe God doesn't want our service. . . ."

In a bold stroke that flies in the face of current thinking on the subject, Michael Green argues that the Great Commission was not a key incentive for evangelism among the early church.

> *A great deal is made in some missionary writings of "the Great Commission" in Matthew 28:18– 20. No doubt this was important. . . . [But] it is quoted very little in the writings of the second century.*[49]

Green goes on to show how the church grounded its appeals for evangelism in the self-sacrificing gift, loving example, and promised presence of Christ. These heroes who served Christ to the point of death "had been gripped by the love of God."

May God increase their tribe.

God doesn't want service that flows out of "duty" any more than my wife wants flowers I brought home "because I'm supposed to." If duty is all you've got for motivation, Grace Deficit Disorder is all you've got for spirituality.

2. A Sense of Responsibility

The earliest disciples' gratitude for Christ lit a fire in their bellies to please him. They were responsible to the Master as stewards of the gospel of grace. They possessed the golden antidote for the world's deadly ailment, and had been sent out by Christ to administer it. They would answer for how they acquitted themselves in that stewardship. For the Christian, final judgment did not determine heaven or hell; that matter had already been settled at salvation. It did, however, determine "the enjoyment of that destiny with God."[50] Their greatest fear was not damnation, but disappointing their "beloved Master" by how they lived as Christians.[51]

They saw their heavenly rewards and capacities for everlasting grace as directly linked to their service for Christ and his gospel. And they supremely saw pleasing Christ as their ultimate responsibility and joy.

Whatever "duty" might have colored the motivations of these earliest Christians was preeminently personal. It was a duty to say thank you to the One who gave his all for them; a privileged opportunity to live every moment of every day in a way that brought a smile to his face.

It's this personal aspect that shields the soul from Grace

Deficit Disorder. To know Jesus, to paint his picture on the corridors of your soul in Scripture-imbued strokes, is to rise above the downward drag of legalism. The doctrine of Christ was never meant to be an end in itself; it is a window opened to fellowship with a true and living person. Doctrine is a means to an end: "that I may know Him..." (Philippians 3:10).

True service for Christ is to be a response to Christ's person more than a duty to Christ's mission. Legalism sucks the *response* out of responsibility.

Green traces how later generations morphed grace into legalism, turning a desire to please Christ into an obligation to earn salvation. That GDD force is ever with us.

But Scripture was clear: you joined Team Jesus by grace through faith, and you continued in grace and faith till the final whistle blew. Sensitive Christ followers understood this.

Why should you serve God in his church?

Because it is your joyful responsibility to please the One who loved you and gave himself up for you. "Therefore we make it our aim, whether present or absent, to be well pleasing to Him" (2 Corinthians 5:9).

3. A Sense of Concern

As a dad of two awesome kids, I find parenting one of the single greatest sources of joy in my life. Even so, the job brings struggles. When my son misses the big tackle on the gridiron, when my daughter struggles with a bully/mean girl at church, when tears roll down their faces, something inside me hurts.

To parent is to carry an ache in your heart. The sun never

sets on my concern for my kids.

The earliest Christians, fueled by the love of Christ, amazed by the grace of God, and inspired by the example of their peers, felt the same ache for a lost and dying world.

When Paul engaged the philosophers on Mars Hill, he described humankind as groping in darkness after God (Acts 17:27). People need hope. People need Christ. People need the gospel.

There's an old preacher story about a good-hearted man who took in a stray dog. He warmed the shivering animal, gently brushed the burrs out of its knotted fur, fed it, and sheltered it for several days. At night, the grateful dog slept at the foot of the man's bed. Over time, the man grew to love the little cur.

One day, he awoke to discover his canine visitor had disappeared. He felt hurt, and then angry. *After all I've done for you, this is the gratitude I get?* He spent a lonely day moping around the house.

The next morning, the man heard scratching at his front door. He ran to open it. The stray was back, happy and excited. Beside him, slouched and shivering, sat a second stray.

One dog telling a second dog where to find food.

When my board members spent that nanosecond wrestling over why anyone should serve God, I wish we had first read Michael Green's analysis:

> *Now if you believe that outside of Christ there*
> *is no hope, it is impossible to possess an atom*
> *of human love and kindness without being*
> *gripped with a great desire to bring men to*

this one way of salvation. We are not surprised, therefore, to find that concern for the state of the unevangelized was one of the great driving forces behind Christian preaching of the gospel in the early Church.[52]

Why should anybody serve God?

Because we care about people.

Because we "possess an atom of human love and kindness."

Because we know life without Christ is harder than it needs to be and eternity without him is unspeakably sad.

Because we want everyone to find the treasure we found when we found Jesus.

Because we're excited to see people we care about be transformed by the love of God.

Because Christ's own love has ignited a fire in our bellies and we can't keep quiet (Romans 5:5).

Or. . .

Because it's our duty? Let me know how that works for you.

God engineered the church to run on the fuel of grace. Any other fuel lets off toxic exhaust. Lost people smell our sputtering engines and scorn our duty-ignited horsepower. Fill the tank with grace. Pure grace. Scandalous grace. Nothing but grace.

Only one life, 'twill soon be past;
Only what's done for Christ will last.[53]

But how much more true this is with one little tweak (and with apologies to the poet):

Only one life, 'twill soon be past.
Only what's done by Christ will last.

Let God do his work, by his power, according to his design, in his own time, through your heart, fueled by high-octane grace, and seized by a muscular faith in the Savior who loved you and gave himself for you.

CHAPTER 9

BOUNCERS

No matter how low down you are; no matter what your disposition has been; you may be low in your thoughts, words, and actions; you may be selfish; your heart may be overflowing with corruption and wickedness; yet Jesus will have compassion upon you. He will speak comforting words to you; not treat you coldly or spurn you, as perhaps those of earth would, but will speak tender words, and words of love and affection and kindness. Just come at once. He is a faithful friend—a friend that sticketh closer than a brother.
D. L. MOODY

"We're sorry," the girl said.

Her friend added, "Yeah, we didn't know."

"What are you talking about?" I asked.

"We came to church on Sunday. . ."

"That's awesome! What did you think?" These two high school girls were excited about God but didn't have their own church. They had come to my youth group, so I invited them to try our church. They told me they'd never been to any church except for a funeral. I was excited they had taken me up on my offer. "So how was it? What did you think?"

"We're so sorry," said one.

"Yeah. We didn't know," said the other.

"What are you talking about?"

"We didn't know we weren't supposed to wear shorts."

They explained how it was hot and muggy—a typical Chicago summer day—and they had planned to go shopping afterward. So they'd worn shorts to church.

An usher "greeted" them on the front steps with these welcoming words: "You can't go in looking like that." So the girls went shopping. Now, at Friday night youth group, they were apologizing to me.

I wanted to punch somebody, in Christian love.

"No! I'm the one who's sorry. You have nothing to be sorry for. That guy was wrong."

Are they ushers or bouncers? Why do some legalists take it as their life's mission to bar the door to God's celestial party? And what does Grace Deficit Disorder do to a soul that makes it so brusque toward outsiders?

Let's probe the legalist/bouncer heart through three case studies.

1. A Narrow Heart: Jonah

Jonah, God's prophet, preferred death to the idea of the Assyrians encountering the grace of God. Narrow-minded. Provincial. Parochial. Racist. He constricted the wideness of God's mercy to a measly trickle for the well-deserving few.

This attitude got him eaten by a giant creature of the sea.

It also earned him the distinction of being the world's first human pile of vomit on the beach.

When he finally preached to the Assyrians, his sermons were nothing but hellfire and brimstone. God used him anyway—proving it's neither the messenger nor the message as much as the God who reaches out.

> *The people of Nineveh believed God's message, and from the greatest to the least, they declared a fast and put on burlap to show their sorrow. When the king of Nineveh heard what Jonah was saying, he stepped down from his throne and took off his royal robes. He dressed himself in burlap and sat on a heap of ashes. Then the king and his nobles sent this decree throughout the city: "No one, not even the animals from your herds and flocks, may eat or drink anything at all. People and animals alike must wear garments of mourning, and everyone must pray earnestly to God. They must turn from their evil ways and stop all their violence. Who can tell? Perhaps even yet God will change his mind and hold back his fierce anger from destroying us." (Jonah 3:5–9 NLT)*

Good news, right?

Not to the legalist. GDD causes a kind of insanity in which the soul's polarities are reversed. What should cause grief—the damnation of souls—causes joy. What should cause joy—the forgiveness of sins and release from condemnation—causes grief.

Jonah was so ticked off, he asked to die. He complained that God showed grace to the Assyrians. He lamented the cancellation of their destruction. The idea that grace might actually be given to these people made him semi-suicidal (Jonah 4:2–3).

God enacted a little parable with a shade plant to convict his sulking prophet and bring him back home to grace.

Nothing outshines God's grace; it is a radiant star against an ink-black sky. Incomparable in beauty, peerless in worth, unparalleled in history—if grace doesn't make your heart skip a beat, at least once in a while, you don't get it yet.

On the cross, Jesus stretched his arms open wide. Wider than any one nation or ethnic group. Wider than any one epoch or age. Wider than you think he did.

His grace extends as wide as the world, for any and all who believe, no matter how evil, how cruel, how vicious, how unworthy.

God help us if we, who are sent by God to a lost and dying world, should ever be found constricting the way to grace and the heaven it brings.

2. A Judgmental Heart: The Elder Brother

Prodigal means out of bounds, excessive, and extreme. That's how bad the prodigal son was in Jesus' parable (Luke 15:11–32). Jesus portrayed a pierced, tattooed, lice-ridden, spiked, strung-out, STD-risking son in all his "gory," and invited us to dislike him.

He also invited us to marvel at the heart of a father who

would not only forgive but who would humiliate himself by running to his son in public. Even deeper, the father wastes more of his already spoiled estate in throwing a party for the undeserving son, complete with prime beef on the spit.

And dancing.

Enter, the elder brother.

He heard the party, got the scoop from one of the servants, and threw a legalistic hissy fit. He wouldn't go in. Instead, he said to his father,

> *"Lo, these many years I have been serving you;*
> *I never transgressed your commandment at any*
> *time; and yet you never gave me a young goat,*
> *that I might make merry with my friends. But as*
> *soon as this son of yours came, who has devoured*
> *your livelihood with harlots, you killed the fatted*
> *calf for him." (Luke 15:29–30)*

Finally, his father came out and *begged him*. If that doesn't fracture your picture of a harsh Almighty God, nothing will.

Let's take the elder brother's litany of accusations one at a time.

Lo, these many years I have been serving you.

He uses the Greek word *douleo*, which is ironic because Christ said he came to serve, not to be served (Mark 10:45). The heart and soul of legalism are found in this exact reversal of roles: "God, I have been serving you. Look at all I've done."

When you really understand grace, your service for God fades into invisibility. His eternity of service for you takes center stage. The father fed, subsidized, housed, loved, blessed, and employed this unappreciative son. Who's the servant in the story?

The elder brother's GDD blinded him to the countless ways his father served him every single day. Jesus underscored the insanity of the elder brother's attitude by having him launch his diatribe with the word *Lo*. *Lo* means *behold*, *look*, or *shine the spotlight here*. Right here, not on what you've done for me, but on what I've done for you.

I never transgressed your commandment at any time.

Right. I once counseled a sex-addicted man who had slept with more women than he could count. He wanted me to know, however, that he rarely looked at porn. In his mind, looking at porn was worse than fornicating.

The self-justifying gene serves as a sure marker for legalism. The truth is, we're all sinners, and the difference between us and the prodigal son is a difference of degree, not of kind. Legalism is simply polished debauchery. And the self-righteous superiority it exudes bars the door against heartbroken people who feel their brokenness.

And yet you never gave me a young goat, that I might make merry with my friends.

Liar. The dad says as much: "All that I have is yours" (Luke 15:31). And the kid knew it.

Here, Jesus cracks the door of one of legalism's darkest secrets. *Legalists feel ripped off by God.* They feel entitled to more than they've received. They genuinely believe God owes them. They have laced up their stiff working boots and wonder when payday's coming. They resent the blessings of others—especially of the "undeserving"—because they themselves have worked harder, they've followed the rules, they've done everything right. Where's their reward?

In all of this, they conveniently forget the massive stacks of blessings the Father lays on them day by day.

But as soon as this son of yours came...

Notice it's not "this brother of mine"; no, it's "this son of yours." Until legalists stand shoulder-to-shoulder with the dregs of humanity and call them brother and embrace them as sister, they can never be set free. Imagine the entire human race crowded before God. He calls two people forward: the prodigal son (before his turnaround), and the Son of God. Then God says, "Everybody, go stand in line behind the person you resemble the most, morally speaking. Ready, go!"

Which line would you stand in? The elder brother refuses to identify with the prodigal at all. Such GDD is fatal. Such legalism bars the doors to repentant prodigals because "they're not good enough for grace." Or because they're wearing shorts. Honestly?

Who has devoured your livelihood with harlots...

Aren't we all living off of God's livelihood? Aren't we all devourers of the bounties of heaven? So, one devours with sexual stimulation, another devours with materialism, yet another devours with good things like hard work and making a living.

Even so, the Father's lament continues through the ages: *"Child, you are always with me, but you don't believe."*

The fact that we all use blessings from the hand of God to move our hearts away from him lands us squarely in the infested sandals of the prodigal son. Even if we're working the Father's fields. When it comes to snubbing God, any seductive force is as destructive as the next. The only difference between the elder brother and his prodigal sibling was geography.

You killed the fattened calf for him.

And he killed it for the elder brother, too, if he'd only get over himself and join the party. The implied accusation is clear: You killed the fattened calf for him and you shouldn't have. He didn't deserve it. Hadn't earned it. Big mistake, Father. And you didn't kill it for me, and I deserved it. I worked hard for it. I merited it.

Whether the sin *du jour* was harlotry, or materialism, or wearing short shorts, or disco dancing, makes no difference. God's Son was slain that "whosoever will" might join the celestial celebration. Sometimes, you just have to cut loose and party with faith's unworthy partyers.

Even "an atom of human love and kindness" in the elder brother's heart would have made him run inside and welcome his little bro home.

3. An Injudicious Heart: Imitators

"I stick a Tootsie Roll in my lip," he said.

"A what? Where? Why?" I said.

"Well, the guys in my community all chew tobacco, and I don't. So the Tootsie Roll turns my spit brown. I can relate to them better that way," he said.

"Oh," I said.

He was a young pastor in the rural Northeast—to a tribe of pickup-trucking, flannel-shirting, tobacco-chewing rednecks. In the spirit of becoming "all things to all people," my pastor friend took up the Tootsie Roll habit to better relate to the men he wanted to reach.

I love that spirit, but I'm not so sure about that practice.

Aside from the risk of getting busted—"Hey Jimmy Bob, got a plug of chaw?" "Nah, have a Tootsie Roll"—there might be a flaw in the logic. Being relevant does not necessarily mean coloring your spit, faux-hawking what's left of your hair, or sporting hipster glasses. It does not require Eminem on your iPod or a misspelled Hebrew tat on your forearm.

Being relevant means being yourself while connecting with a tribe that's different from yours, and offering them hope for a way out their fallen condition.

Could it be you don't need to copy the world to save the world?

This is the neo-legalist's particular challenge.

Evangelical icon D. Martyn Lloyd-Jones argued that people are looking for a way out of their broken condition. They're not looking for someone who is like them, but *unlike* them. Someone who offers deliverance from, not immersion into, the fallen lifestyle they're stuck in. Lloyd-Jones points out, "Our Lord attracted sinners because he was different."[54]

You don't have to completely imitate the people you're trying to reach; in their heart of hearts, they're trying to imitate you—when you're at your best.

The prodigal's father could have slaughtered the fattened calf and personally delivered prime beef to his son in the far country at any time. He could have thrown a party there, right where the son was making a pig of himself. He could have dressed and spoken the language of that faraway land. But he didn't.

If grace means niceness, if grace means unconditional love, if grace means injudicious dispensing of snacks to slackers, then why not party with the prodigals while still in the far country, to reach them better? Why wait for them to come to their senses? Why wait for them to come home?

Go to them. Go be them. Right?

Not so fast.

Our Father loves prodigals too much to subsidize their self-destructive behaviors. He wants his wayward kids to bottom out ASAP, because that's the only way grace will be received as power-to-come-home and not as feeding-the-far-country-monster.

In an ultimate irony, the sentiment that confuses grace with indifference toward sin winds up barring the door to the very grace we hope to offer. Why exit the pig sty if grace makes pig sties okay? Sometimes "unconditional" becomes code for "it doesn't matter."

But it does matter. Because God longs to deliver us from our lies. He insists we see "the good life" in terms other than money, sex, power, drugs, booze, rock and roll, religion, health, wealth, and the American dream.

And maybe that's evangelism's un-dirty little secret: You don't have to become prodigal to reach prodigals. You don't have to party to reach partyers. Speak their language, yes. Love the sinner, yes. Enter their world, absolutely.

But don't get stuck on the world's flypaper.

Be different. Offer the lost tribe a way out. Incarnate a countercultural remedy for their current broken lifestyle. Maybe the flannel-shirted rednecks didn't need to see someone whose spit was brown as much as someone who was happy and normal with moderately clear spit. Without Christ, what people have isn't working for them; so, be the alternative.

Grace delivered you from the sewer and showered you clean.

Now help the next guy out.

Clearing the Way Home

"Divide the land the LORD your God is giving you into three districts, with one of these cities in each district. Then anyone who has killed someone can flee to one of the cities of refuge for safety." (Deuteronomy 19:3 NLT)

The ancient Jewish legal system provided an escape hatch for accidental criminals. If a lumberjack's ax head flew off and killed his neighbor, the neighbor's family had a right to kill the lumberjack. But there was an out: he could flee to a designated city of refuge and be safe.

The Jews were to keep the roads to their cities of refuge in good repair. A third-degree murderer running for his life, fleeing from justice and racing toward mercy, shouldn't have to jump over a stream or trip over a twig on the way. He was on a highway of grace, and the priests were supposed to keep it clean.

God help us if we—a kingdom of priests charged with clearing the way to eternal refuge (Hebrews 6:18)—should ever toss marbles on the road.

Grace doesn't need bouncers; it needs inviters.

"Go out into the highways and hedges, and compel them to come in," Jesus said (Luke 14:23). Don't take no for an answer unless you have to. And don't stand there blocking the way.

In grace, Christ stretched his arms as wide as the human race. Rich and poor. Morally high and morally low. Slave and free.

Every member of God's family must be so gospel-wise that we do nothing to make any sinner feel unqualified to come to Christ. Sinfulness, in fact, is the essential qualification—Jesus didn't come for the righteous, but for sinners.

Let them come in. Even if they're wearing shorts. Or skorts. Or lice-infested dreadlocks. Or an Armani suit. Or tattered rags.

Let the whole race of prodigals join the celestial feast.

CHAPTER 10

THE CROSS

All heaven is interested in the cross of Christ,
all hell terribly afraid of it, while men are the only
beings who more or less ignore its meaning.
OSWALD CHAMBERS (1800s)

"Keep your mouth shut."

"Don't say a word."

"Don't tell anybody about me."

In a weirdly anti-evangelistic move, Jesus often told exuberant followers to keep their mouths shut about him.

After healing a leper, Jesus said, "See that you tell no one" (Matthew 8:4).

After declaring he would build his church, "He commanded his disciples that they should tell no one that He was Jesus the Christ" (Matthew 16:20).

When he restored hearing and speech to a man born deaf and mute, "He commanded them that they should tell no one; but the more He commanded them, the more widely they proclaimed it" (Mark 7:36).

After raising a little girl from the dead, Jesus "charged [her parents] to tell no one what had happened" (Luke 8:56).

Why all the secrecy? Why would the same Lord who sent his disciples to preach the gospel to every creature issue so many warnings to keep mum? Scholars debate the motive behind this Messianic Secret, as it's known. But Jesus left some clues.

The most important clue comes from a similar oddity in Mark's Gospel. Peter, James, and John had just finished a mind-blowing encounter called the Transfiguration—a mini-preview of Christ in his future glory. "Now as they came down from the mountain, He [Jesus] commanded them that they should tell no one the things they had seen, till the Son of Man had risen from the dead" (Mark 9:9).

Don't let the secret out, Jesus said, till he had risen from the dead. Then, let 'er rip.

Why?

Because you don't know Jesus until you grasp the basics of his Cross and Resurrection. So please keep your mouth shut until then, thank you. The partial portrait does more damage than good.

Prime example: those who wanted to make Jesus king by force. Is Jesus king? Yes. Was the Messiah coming to rule the earth? Yes.

So why not overthrow Rome and make him king?

In one breath: because Jesus wasn't coming to be king in that way and at that time, because his Kingdom isn't by force, and his Kingship begins in the heart, and the heart is fallen; so for Jesus to rule there, he must first redeem it, but before he can redeem it, he must first atone for sins, thus reconciling fallen humans to God, thereby triggering the chain reaction eventuating in Jesus being King, in one life at a time, till he returns.

Get all that?

Awesome. Because then it makes sense for Jesus to verbally body slam those who would make him king by acclamation. And it makes equal sense for him to armlock those who would depict him as anything without painting that anything in the primary colors of Crucifixion and Resurrection.

Are you excited about a miracle? Great! But don't talk about it until you can frame that miracle within the death and Resurrection of the Savior.

Are you fired up for finding lost people? Great! But stay home until you can proclaim "Jesus Christ and him crucified" as the hope of every broken heart (1 Corinthians 2:2).

Are you ready to do something to heal the world's wounds? Great! But make sure the balm you apply—the water you supply, the medical help you offer, or the emotional support you render—overflows with a crucified Savior.

Don't tell anybody anything until you've graduated through the fundamentals of the Cross and the Resurrection.

Until you have everlasting good news... *Shhh.*

Open your eyes to a Savior, bloodied but unbowed, wounded for you, reconciling lost people to God. Put on Cross-colored glasses, because all those exciting miracles Jesus did, and all those healings he performed, and all those kindnesses he offered, and all those teachings he taught were nothing but pointers to this awful, wonderful centerpiece of cosmic history.

Nothing mars the teachings of grace like a distorted portrait of Christ.

This Is a Football

"Gentlemen, this is a football."

Legendary coach of the Green Bay Packers, Vince Lombardi, began preseason training with those immortal words. Before him sat seasoned veterans, some who'd played football all their lives. As starry-eyed kids, they had slept with footballs clutched in their arms, dreaming of the day they'd make the big leagues. They knew what a football looked like.

That didn't stop Coach Lombardi. He held one up and returned to ground zero of the game. By drilling the basics over and over again, Lombardi transformed a team of perpetual losers into a football dynasty.

What is our football as Christians?

The Cross.

Says who? Says the one who commanded his people to keep on "showing the Lord's death till he comes" through the Lord's Supper. The one recurring ritual that Jesus left to the church was a flashing neon sign pointing to the Cross.

The early apostles got the message.

1 Corinthians 2:2: I determined not to know anything among you except Jesus Christ and Him crucified.

Galatians 6:14: God forbid that I should boast except in the cross of our Lord Jesus Christ, by whom the world has been crucified to me, and I to the world.

1 Corinthians 1:22–23: Jews request a sign, and Greeks seek after wisdom; but we preach Christ crucified, to the Jews a stumbling block and to the Greeks foolishness.

Of all the big deals in theology, the biggest deal is the Cross of Christ and all it means. Grace rests on the Cross like an old hound dog rests on a blanket. So Jesus gathered his ragtag followers and turned a Passover meal into an endless commemoration of that dark day soon to dawn.

Jesus is into commemorating because we are into forgetting. Never forget, he said.

So. . .this is the Cross.

We will contemplate it in two parts: "Christ died" (history), and "for our sins" (theology).

Christ Died (History)

Pretty gold crosses dangling on shiny chains have a narcotic effect on our thoughts about the Cross. So do two thousand years and five thousand miles of distance. Our sanitized crosses fall far short of the gut-wrenching realities of crucifixion. What the Gospels say in four icy words, "and they crucified Him" (Mark 15:25), would have been emotionally devastating to behold, much less endure.

What happened to a crucified person?

Medical experts have reconstructed the physiological effects of this horrific Roman death by torture. Though they don't all agree on the precise cause of death, they all affirm agonies beyond comprehension.

The scourging. Again, the Gospel writers assert the event in stark terms: "Pilate took Jesus and scourged Him" (John 19:1). To scourge means to skin alive with a whip. The beating was made worse by animal bones or lead weights embedded in the whip's tails. Sometimes the weights were pointed, a type of whip called *scorpiones*. The naked victim would suffer intense pain on the chest, back, backside, and groin. Deep bruising would quickly turn to open lacerations and rib fractures often caused "bouts of vomiting tremors, seizures, and fainting fits."[55]

The crown of thorns and other tortures. The agony deepened.

> *They clothed Him with purple; and they twisted a crown of thorns, put it on His head, and began to salute Him, "Hail, King of the Jews!" Then they struck Him on the head with a reed and spat on Him; and bowing the knee, they worshiped Him. (Mark 15:17–19)*

Most likely, the crown of thorns would have been shaped like a cap (not a circlet, as is often portrayed in paintings of the Crucifixion), with sharp spikes everywhere on the top of Jesus' head.[56] Matthew explains that the soldiers "took the reed and struck Him on the head" (Matthew 27:30), in effect hammering the spikes into Christ's scalp. The pain would have been excruciating.

Still think *grace* means *leniency?*

This is the brutal reality of the Cross.

They also spit on him (Matthew 27:30), blindfolded him, took turns punching him in the face (Luke 22:64), and possibly tore out his beard (Isaiah 50:6).

Next time you partake of that little piece of bread in the Lord's Supper that represents Christ's body "which is broken for you" (1 Corinthians 11:24), give some thought to the savage depths those words held for Jesus.

The nails. The spikes were made of iron, and about four-and-a-half inches long.[57] In 1968, archaeologists unearthed a gruesome death chamber: men, women, and children who died by violent means. One of the victims, whose name, Jehohanan, was etched onto his box of bones, clearly died by crucifixion. An iron spike remained through his heel bone. The tip of the spike was bent, most likely from hitting a knot in the wood.[58] The force used in driving the nails would have caused searing pain throughout the body.

Given what Jesus had already endured, his body would fail quickly. Shock would be inevitable.

Crucifixion remains one of the most brutal tortures ever devised by depraved human hearts.

Zugibe states,

> *Following these insults [i.e., the tortures preceding the cross], He was in a severely exhausted condition, experiencing ubiquitous pains, and in a state of increasing shock. The pains would have been unrelenting and brutal, causing severe burning sensations all over His body.*[59]

This is the Cross.

"This is My body which was broken for you." Jesus wants us to look at that moment. To remember it. Contemplate it. Never forget it.

"Broken."

"For you."

Scholars disagree on how the cross would have been

stood upright. In any event, as soon as the body's full weight transferred to the nails through his hands and feet, Christ's already horrific pain would have been magnified to levels beyond words.

Yet, none of this compared to the pains about to come.

Breathing and breaking the legs. Some experts suggest that breathing would have become an immediate problem, requiring a victim of crucifixion to push up on his nail-pierced feet in order to breathe. While this is debated, it is clear that breaking the victim's legs with clubs would easily hasten shock and death.[60] When the Romans came to break Christ's legs, he had already died (John 19:33).

This is the Cross, the fountainhead of all grace. If you don't know the Cross of Christ, you don't know grace.

Death. What was the ultimate cause of Christ's death? Medical experts offer various theories, including a ruptured heart, asphyxiation, or hypovolemic shock from loss of blood.

John, in his Gospel, offered his inspired theory.

> *So when Jesus had received the sour wine, He said,*
> *"It is finished!" And bowing His head, He gave up*
> *His spirit. (John 19:30)*

Let's reserve the theology behind "It is finished!" for the next section, and zero in on the words *He gave up his spirit.*

D. A. Carson links this statement with Christ's earlier in-your-face announcement: "No one takes [my life] from Me, but I lay it down of Myself. I have power to lay it down, and I have power to take it again" (John 10:18).[61] The idea is that Christ died when he was good and ready. He relinquished his spirit. He gave up his life by choice.

Gerald Borchert comments,

> *Jesus is portrayed as totally in control of the*
> *time of his dying, just as he had been pictured*
> *as in control of his arrest, his appearance before*
> *Annas, his trial before the spineless Pilate, and the*
> *carrying of his own cross. For his readers John was*
> *illustrating in bold letters that even what seems to*
> *be tragedy was still not out of God's control.*[62]

Jesus was nobody's victim.

He finished his work and dismissed his spirit.

The two little words, "Christ died," pack enough punch to send the devil tumbling head over heels across the cosmos forever. The next time you partake of the Communion cup and bread, stop and take a breath. Bring your mind back to that awful day. Block everything out long enough to remember the Lord's brutal death.

Especially block out insipid devotionals about something you should do for God, or any off-topic commentary diverting your attention from the bloodied Savior.

This is the fountainhead of all grace. This is the Cross.

This is what God did for you.

There's nothing you can say about Jesus that makes sense apart from this. There is nothing so heartbreaking as the old rugged cross. No moment at once so terrible and so full of hope. Whatever else we may say about the problem of human suffering, no one can accuse God of standing aloof from it. He entered into our pain to a depth that knows no bounds. He felt what we feel and more.

No wonder the early apostles proclaimed, "God forbid that I should boast except in the cross of our Lord Jesus Christ" (Galatians 6:14).

Christ died for our sins.

Christ died. That is history. If you had been there, you could have seen it.

Christ died *for our sins.* That is theology. That requires a word from God. What did his death mean?

For Our Sins (Theology)

The physical sufferings were not the most painful part of Christ's death. Through them all, he didn't cry out, didn't scream, and didn't complain. "As a sheep before its shearers is silent, so He opened not His mouth" (Isaiah 53:7).

But then something happened so breathtakingly horrible that Jesus cried out.

What could be more painful than the tortures, the beatings, the crown of thorns, and the nails through his hands and feet?

Our sins.

When our sins were laid upon him, that's when Jesus cried out.

> *About the ninth hour Jesus cried out with a loud voice, saying, "Eli, Eli, lama sabachthani?" that is, "My God, My God, why have You forsaken Me?"*
> *(Matthew 27:46)*

For Jesus, no physical suffering compared to being

forsaken by God—a black-box mystery, a breach in the eternal fellowship between Christ on the cross and his Father in heaven. This is impenetrable darkness. Bow in wonder and keep silent.

Why did God forsake him?

Because God was judging him for the sin of the world. Damning him. Condemning him. Christ died for our sins. For *my* sins. For *yours*.

He died not as a victim, but as a volunteer.

Leon Morris, in his definitive study *The Apostolic Preaching of the Cross*, described the heartbeat of this good news in seven concepts that, when understood, will send religion's house of cards crashing down and will deliver souls once and for all from the sweatshop of human performance.[63] I suggest using these concepts—or any similar list—as a primer for gospel rookies. Let's dig into the meat of the gospel and our so-great salvation.

Here's the theological side of the Cross, following Morris's outline:

1. Redemption. The shed blood of Christ purchased you for God from the slave market of sin. By that great ransom, Christ set you free from every form of bondage: from sin, legalism, Satan, death, hell, and the grave. This spiritual freedom tees up the ball for your emotional freedom, meaning ongoing deliverance from addiction, despair, and all the messy stuff of your fallen existence. Redemption is the foundation of true Christian liberty. *Key words:* freedom, liberty, ransom, purchase, price. *Key Scriptures:* Acts 20:28; Hebrews 9:12; Galatians 4:4–5; 1 Corinthians 1:30; 1 Peter 1:18–19.

2. Covenant. By the Cross of Christ, God signed in blood the testament of grace, guaranteeing a breathtaking inheritance for all the undeserving heirs. He bound himself in a covenant of love, promising you peace, provision, security, protection, and blessings so glorious, they'd fry the circuits of an unregenerate heart. He became your Father, your Husband, your Defender, and your King. The burden of the covenant lies on his shoulders; the blessings of the covenant flow to yours. *Key words:* promise, oath, earnest, guarantee, blessing. *Key Scriptures:* Deuteronomy 7:9; Psalm 89:34; Jeremiah 31:31–33; Hebrews 7:22, 8:6, 13:20.

3. The Blood. The blood of Christ, a symbol of life outpoured and a violent death endured, embraces everything Jesus did to reconcile you to God. By this blood, you've been redeemed (1 Peter 1:18–19), reconciled (Colossians 1:20), forgiven (Ephesians 1:7), brought near to God (Ephesians 2:13), cleansed in conscience (Hebrews 9:14), been made satisfactory to God (by propitiation, Romans 3:25), and declared good enough for God forever (by justification, Romans 5:9).

It was his death—not his life, not his teachings, not his miracles, not his love—that shoved darkness into a bottomless pit and rescued your sorry soul forever. Yes, these wonders of the life of Christ dazzle angels and demons, yet they were nothing if not a prelude to his death. Any Christian who can't easily connect the dots between the events of Christ's death and the meaning of salvation has a whole lot of growing to do. *Key words:* sacrifice, death, Crucifixion, offering, Cross. *Key Scriptures:* 1 Peter 1:18–19; Ephesians 1:7; Romans 3:25.

4. The Lamb of God. Twice in his Gospel, John calls Jesus "the Lamb of God," adding "who takes away the sin of the world" (John 1:29, 36). I'd like to point out that "sin" is singular—the entirety of your sin viewed en masse. Though the precise Old Testament connection is uncertain, the Lamb of God most surely spotlights Jesus-as-Sacrificial-Substitute. Morris writes:

> *In Jesus Christ there is fulfilled all that is foreshadowed in all the sacrifices. The term is sacrificial. . . . He is the complete embodiment of all the truth to which the sacrificial system pointed.*[64]

Key words: substitute, vicarious, sacrifice, spotless, sinless, peace, forgiveness, Passover. *Key Scriptures:* John 1:29, 36; Exodus 12; John 19:14; 1 Corinthians 5:7; Genesis 22:7–8, Acts 8:32; 1 Peter 1:19.

5. *Propitiation.* God, by nature, cannot be satisfied with sinners. Christ, by dying, fixed that. The more I study the word *propitiation*, the more I fall in love with the truth behind it, and the more I grieve its near disappearance from the Christian lexicon. Nothing heals legalism's scars like the balm of propitiation. God is satisfied with you. He isn't hacked off at you. He isn't disappointed. Isn't hurtling lightning bolts your way, and isn't even tempted. No sighs, no head shakes, no eye rolls. Just an endless smile of just-as-you-are satisfaction, on account of Calvary love, from a Father who calls you "the apple of his eye" (Psalm 17:8). *Key words:* satisfied, accepted, wrath, mercy seat. *Key Scriptures:* 1 John 2:2; 4:10; Romans 3:25; Hebrews 2:17.

6. *Reconciliation.* God finds you as his enemy; he makes you his friend. He finds you estranged and alienated, like warring parties in a nasty divorce, and he makes you reconciled, with more love than ever before. Reconciliation

is God's way of making peace with sinners. How? "Having made peace through the blood of His cross" (Colossians 1:20). There was no other way. Morris writes, "Scripture is clear that reconciliation between God and man could be brought about only by the death of the Son of God."[65] *Key words:* peace, alienated, brought near, enmity, hostility, atonement. *Key Scriptures:* Romans 5:10; 2 Corinthians 5:18–20; Colossians 1:20–21.

7. *Justification.* Perhaps the most important, and least understood, play in the divine playbook, justification stands sentry over the grace of the gospel. Tied as much to Christ's Resurrection as to his Crucifixion, justification sets the table for Christianity's most powerful non-paradox: God justifies the ungodly. How? By what logic can the consuming fire of divine holiness declare ungodly people good enough for God?

Only by the logic of substitution.

Only by the scandal of the Cross (1 Corinthians 1:21).

On that cross, Christ subtracted my sins, bringing me up from the hole I'd dug all the way to ground zero.

By his Resurrection, Christ added his own righteousness to my account—his own goodness-good-enough-for-God, lifting me from zero to heaven.

Justification proves that what God demands, God provides. He demands full payment for sin, and he provided that in the awful cross. He demands perfect righteousness to stand in his presence, and he provided that, too. So God is just *and* the justifier of whosoever believes on Jesus (Romans 3:26), even if that whosoever is a good-for-nothing loser. Because, in reality, when compared to Jesus, aren't we all that way? Yes, God justifies the ungodly; who else is there? *Key words:*

righteous, righteousness, just, condemnation, wrath, forensic, legal, federal head, substitution, impute, reckon, substitution. *Key Scriptures:* Romans 3–4; Genesis 15:6; Romans 8:33–34; 2 Corinthians 5:21; Galatians 3–4.

This is the Cross. This is the Savior. This is salvation. This is a gift, a grace, a boundless love, a gospel, a truth worth fighting for, and the truth a lost and dying world so desperately needs to hear.

The church in our day needs a fresh awakening to these old truths. We need to sink deep roots into the glories of the atonement, that the Holy Spirit might create an impregnable fortress of grace in our souls.

The more deeply we know a truth, the more easily we can explain it to someone else. As often as we eat this bread and drink this cup, we proclaim the Lord's death, until he comes.

> *On a hill, far away, stood an old, rugged Cross,*
> *The emblem of suff'ring and shame,*
> *And I love that old cross, where the Dearest and Best,*
> *For a world of lost sinners was slain.*[66]

Christ died: what an unspeakably brutal fact! *For our sins:* what jaw-dropping wonders! When the author of Hebrews declares, "It is good that the heart be established by grace" (Hebrews 13:9), he invites us to build our entire lives on the bedrock truths flowing from the Cross.

That's because the doctrines of grace will build a mighty fortress in your soul, if you study them. You have to drill them, like a quarterback drills footwork or a pianist drills arpeggios. What if every Christ follower were so wise in the gospel that any mention of the Cross conjured an indestructible edifice of grace truths so interlocked that no amount of huffing and puffing—whether it be demonic, psychotic, or from SCOWL's harshest taskmasters—could ever blow it down?

This is the Cross. Let us apply our hearts to its treasures in ever-deepening measure, and then open our mouths to speak forth its worth.

> *He hell in hell laid low;*
> *Made sin, he sin o'erthrew;*
> *Bowed to the grave, destroyed it so,*
> *And death, by dying, slew.*[67]

CHAPTER 11

SANCTIFICATION

How easy, how spontaneous, how delightful this heavenly way of holiness! Surely it is a "highway" and not the low way of man's vain and fruitless mortification. It is God's great elevated railway, sweeping over the heads of the struggling throngs who toil along the lower road when they might be borne along on His ascension pathway by His own almighty impulse. It is God's great elevator carrying us up to the higher chambers of His palace, without arduous efforts, while others struggle up the winding stairs and faint by the way.[68]
A. B. SIMPSON (1800s)

It isn't hard to wring your hands over the moral condition of our culture and of the church. SCOWL likes to lay this problem at the feet of dangerous "hyper-grace" preachers. If we'd quit giving Christians a hall pass to sin, they say, the church would get holy. There's a defect in the hyper-grace gospel, they say, so there's unholiness woven into hyper-grace converts.

I'd like to suggest that the opposite is actually the truth.

Whatever unholiness we see in the church is mainly Grace Deficit Disorder running amok. Unholiness results from legalism (Matthew 23:28). When temptation rears its ugly head, your sanctification will only be as strong as your justification feels real. You can't be holy until you can link Christ's victory at Calvary to your victory in temptation.

Sadly, there's not one in a hundred Christians who understands the connection, and therefore most are doomed to grope in darkness toward legalistic versions of holiness.

It is time for God's people to rise up in a heartfelt holiness to God. It is time for cleansing to come to the household of faith. Holiness is what the church so urgently needs.

But not a grunt-it-out holiness. Not a Westboro Baptist holiness. Not an activist Martha-in-the-kitchen holiness. Not a Camazotzian/Stepford holiness, either. Wherever holiness emerges from mere human effort, wherever it is a work of the flesh, wherever it parrots some preacher's neo-legalistic agenda or a traditional-legalist's denouncements, wherever it is a holiness of scruples, or rules, or regulations, it will be as bogus as a busted politician's crocodile tears.

The real deal can only thrive in the overflow of grace. Here are some essential truths of grace-oriented sanctification.

Sanctification, Grace Style

1. Sanctification only flows out of union with Christ.

In the exact moment of your salvation, God joined you to Christ. He super-glued you to Jesus, and you became one with him. The Bible calls this being "in Christ" or "in him." Union with Christ is the heartbeat of sanctification.

You have been so united to Christ that everything that is true of Jesus Christ in his humanity before the Father has now become true of you.

Let that seep through your legalistic crust.

His history is yours: you died with Christ (Romans 6:1–4).

His destiny is yours: you will one day light up the cosmos as a dazzling spectacle, sharing the glory of Christ (Colossians 3:4; 1 John 3:2).

His possessions are yours: you are a joint heir with Jesus, with the secret code to unlock heaven's vaults—the whispered name of the Savior (Ephesians 2:7, 3:8).

His status is yours: since he is royal, you are royal. Since he is heir, you are heir. Since he has authority, you have authority. Since he is righteous, you are righteous (Ephesians 1:11, 3:12; Philippians 3:9).

His nature (in his humanity) is yours, too: Is he powerful? You are powerful. Is Christ holy? You are holy, too. You've been "perfected forever" (Hebrews 10:14). You were a moral catastrophe, but "you were washed, but you were sanctified, but you were justified in the name of the Lord Jesus and by the Spirit of our God" (1 Corinthians 6:11). Until you see yourself sanctified in Christ, nobody will ever see you sanctified in life.

You are a saint, not a sinner. You're not even a sinner saved by grace, technically speaking. What you *are* is what Christ, in his human nature before the Father, is. And while it may be humility that makes you say, "I'm just a worthless sinner saved by grace," it is a needless humility and it isn't truth. Even worse, the "I'm just a sinner" statement creates a self-fulfilling prophecy. Your lifestyle will inevitably incarnate whatever self-identifying labels you embrace.

I don't want to create a reverse legalism here by pounding on the head of anybody who says "I'm just an old rotten sinner saved by grace," but I do want to challenge the cliché.

That's what you *were*, but it's not what you *are*.

What you *are* is a saint, a holy one, saved by grace and sanctified by grace, too.

Everything important to your Christianity starts here. Until you can say, "I am one with Christ," you're going to make sanctification a miserable process. It will always feel like you're trying to make something happen; like you're straining for a pretty ribbon that some jerk keeps moving out of reach.

But it is within reach because you're joined to Christ, and nothing is out of reach for him.

2. You don't serve God for *blessing, you only serve him* from *blessing.*

On day one of your salvation, you received every blessing you'll ever receive. Your birthright became yours. Your divine riches became yours. Your spiritual portfolio of divine assets— enough to last you a lifetime and beyond—became yours, in full, the moment you first believed.

You are as blessed as you can be, and as blessed as you'll ever be, from that moment on. God has "blessed us with every spiritual blessing in heavenly places in Christ" (Ephesians 1:3). Notice the past tense; it's a done deal.

Peter says, "His divine power has given to us all things that pertain to life and godliness" (2 Peter 1:3). Let's just give a little love to that word *all*. All the pieces of sanctification's puzzle are not only sitting on the table, they're being assembled by the Spirit of Christ in you every single day.

The Christian life is a God-blessed life, by definition. It is not your task to get blessed; it's your privilege to unwrap the blessings that are already yours; to experience the grace that's already been given; or, as old-timers used to say, to possess your possessions.

As a pastor, if I want you to be holy, the best thing I can do for you is to teach you about the riches you already have in Christ. Explain to you your privileges. Show you what rights you have. Uncover your glories. Persuade you, from God's Word, of your incredible new identity in him.

Everywhere I go, Christians are up to speed with their duties and sadly ignorant of their privileges. GDD owns their emotions. Instead of standing in their blessings, they slouch in their failures. They wind up either faking holiness, beating themselves up over unholiness, or bitterly trashing the whole idea and just giving up. Another casualty of the doctrine of demons called legalism.

Don't fall for it.

You are already blessed.

God won't bless you more if you pray hard. He won't bless you more if you read your Bible more. He won't bless you more if you jettison a sin from your life, or if you build a hospital in Africa.

Those are all very good things, but not one is the ground of your blessing.

You are blessed because God blesses Jesus Christ and you are in Christ. He blesses you for Christ's sake.

You are blessed on good days and bad. On your holy days and unholy days. When you feel blessed and when you don't. You are blessed.

To whatever degree you harbor the lunacy that you are going to serve God for a blessing, you have confused receiving grace with earning a paycheck.

God doesn't give paychecks.

He gives blessings, free and clear, in Christ alone.

In fact, when you understand grace, you realize that any good works you might squeeze out are themselves the blessings of God, a part of salvation's magnificent grace package.

God gave you your blessings, all at once, as a mountain of beautifully wrapped gifts. This happened on salvation's first day for you. Now, go tear into the packages, see what you have, and enjoy each gift, day by day and moment by moment, through faith.

God can't bless you any more than he has already blessed you. Because of Christ, you are the richest person you know. You have everything you need for both your present happiness and your powerful service. You can handle anything that comes your way. You are beloved of God. You are as righteous in his eyes as Jesus Christ himself. You are blessed better than you deserve, but exactly as Christ deserves, and nothing will ever rattle this truth.

Let it sink in: you don't serve God for blessing; you serve him *from* blessing. Whatever you do for God can only thrive in the outflow of what God has first done for you.

3. Sanctification isn't imitation; it's habitation.

Every good thing that happens in and through you happens only through Christ in you. Take away this mystical union, and Christianity cheapens into pop psychology slathered in Jesus quotes.

Just as only God can please God, only Christ can be like Christ. And he intends to do so—to be completely himself—through you.

This means we must radically revise the notion of "imitating Christ." An infant mimics the funny faces her mother makes, but that doesn't work with the heavy lifting needed for the self-sacrificing, sinner-forgiving, people-loving, fear-conquering integrity demonstrated by Christ. We can no more imitate him than we can imitate Mr. Universe bench-pressing a Volkswagen.

Sanctification is not about imitation.

Sanctification is about habitation.

Oswald Chambers writes,

> *The one marvelous secret of a holy life lies not in imitating Jesus, but in letting the perfections of Jesus manifest themselves in my mortal flesh. Sanctification is "Christ in you.". . . Sanctification is not drawing from Jesus the power to be holy; it is drawing from Jesus the holiness that was manifested in Him, and He manifests it in me.*[69]

What is sanctification? It is the indwelling life of Christ shining through you. His heart becomes yours. His love becomes yours. His wholeness, courage, character, truth, and his mission all become yours. In other words, except for hairstyle, clothing, and cultural stuff like flatbread and sandals, you become a whole lot like Jesus.

This doesn't make you a clone. Christ hasn't moved inside you to make you weird. He's not interested in making you something you're not.

He makes you into your truest self, the real you with all the color added. Christ digs away the crud that's accumulated over your heart and lets your dream-self shine through, unfettered by legalism.

Habitation, not imitation.

Jesus Christ did not ransom you from the slave market of sin so you could perform for him by the sweat of your brow. The sweat of sanctification stays on his brow. He is Yahweh Mekeddeshem, the Lord Who Sanctifies You (Exodus 31:13). Paul says, "But of Him you are in Christ Jesus, who became for us. . .sanctification" (1 Corinthians 1:30).

God sees you as holy. God sees you as perfect. God sees you as good enough for him. He is not a picky mother-in-law—never happy, never satisfied—whose only smile is the half smile of chronic disappointment. No. You're beautiful to him because you are beautiful. You are all these things, in reality.

It is only here, on planet Earth, in the land of reality-lite, that you or anybody would ever see you as anything but what God says about you.

As often as you believe what God says about you, your everyday lifestyle will match the permanently sanctified life that has been implanted in you (Ephesians 4:1).

4. Sanctification isn't an attainment; it's an obtainment.

> *I have been crucified with Christ; it is no longer I who live, but Christ lives in me; and the life which I now live in the flesh I live by faith in the Son of God, who loved me and gave Himself for me. (Galatians 2:20)*

Ever since the day of my salvation, the only person walking around earth inside my skin is Bill-plus-Christ. That is my identity. That is my nature. That is my power. Bill-plus-zero is dead. Bill-plus-Christ is alive forevermore.

This crucifixion with Christ provides the secret sauce for a world-class feast of life-changing truth.

I died to my dysfunctional past. I died to my sinner status. I died to my legalistic twitching. I died to Grace Deficit Disorder. Those forces have no power in my life today, except the power of their persuasive lies. They are illusions. Delusions.

As long as truth reigns, those lies stay dead. Faith is the victory. You've died to these things, God says. Believe it, and move on with your life.

You also died to legalism's ladder of perfection. You will not be sanctified by lifting yourself to a higher moral plane. Sanctification is not a trophy given to high achievers after they've expended enough sweat and tears.

Ask yourself a question: *Can I be holy today?* The answer is yes, because Christ is in you. Holiness always lies within reach. You can obtain it in any temptation in any moment on any day.

But what if you were unholy yesterday? What if you bit the juicy apple of nasty sin? Can you be holy today? Yes, again, because Christ is still in you. You have all power to put down the apple and take hold of the sanity and wholeness that is holiness.

You can be holy any hour you choose.

That's because holiness is already in you through the person of Jesus Christ. You didn't *attain* this holiness; you *obtained* it when you received Christ. He brought it with him.

Christ had very high expectations of his disciples. He believed in them more than they believed in themselves. As long as he was with them, anything was possible.

It is the same for you.

You don't need to graduate to levels of holiness. You don't need to wait until you've earned your wings. Sanctification is not an attainment of grueling synergy between your efforts and God's. Because Christ's holiness is an ever-present reality in your life, it is an ever-present potentiality in your lifestyle. The fiercest tempter is no match for Jesus.

Faith flips the switches that actualize your potential. Paul said, "I live by faith in the Son of God." Faith takes God at his word. Faith silences the devil's toothless roar. Faith obtains the promises, and God has promised holiness. Sanctification is not a grueling attainment, it is an organic obtainment, completely natural for a child bearing heaven's DNA.

When your father-in-law snipes, or your lusts beckon, the only reason you might react unrighteously is failure to look to Christ. Immediately, all your old imperfections clamber forth in your memories to claw at your self-worth. So you lash out at the old jerk. But Christ has washed those imperfections away; you have nothing left to prove—look to Christ in faith.

Fears of failure instantly claim ownership of your mind and heart, so you fume and fret and curse. But Christ has dethroned those fears, and failure means nothing to you— look to Christ in faith.

Bitterness from unresolved family drama burns your throat with bile, and you binge on a bag of Oreos. But Christ has defanged those predators—quick! Look to Christ in faith.

An unholy act in your life is not a deficit in your new

nature; it's not a deficit in the character of Christ; it's not a deficit in grace.

It is a deficit in your thinking and believing about all these things. Grace Deficit Disorder. You believed a lie. You put your faith in the wrong claimant. Therefore, you obtained an outcome you regret.

I would rather have you struggle to believe God and act accordingly than struggle not to sin. That's because what you focus on begins to dominate you. To focus on not sinning is to shine the spotlight on sin. Guess what's going to dominate you?

Instead, focus on Christ and his power, Christ and his capabilities, Christ and his invincible love for you, and Christ and his ever-present help in time of trouble.

You can obtain holiness today, if you'll only take God at his word. Never mind your lousy attitude yesterday. You have been sanctified, perfected, washed, empowered, and indwelled by Christ. You may feel weak. You may feel weary. You may feel tempted, and tried, and folded, spindled, and mutilated. Even so, faith always wins. There is no official feeling of the power of God. There is no official feeling of Christ living through you. No matter how you feel, faith is the victory (1 John 5:4). Win the fight of faith, and every other victory falls into place.

Be holy as Christ is holy. Yes, it's possible, one day at a time.

Your job is faith.

Christ's job is living through you.

Never let a legalist's assault bully you from sanctification's bedrock truth: "He who calls you is faithful, who also will do it" (1 Thessalonians 5:24).

Arrows Revisited

Earlier we talked about arrows that show the flow of blessing from God down to you. I did my best to wipe out all the arrows that point from you to God, body slamming pride to the mat, and showing how God does fine without your help.

But that leaves the question unanswered: Is there anything you can do for God? Do any arrows point up?

Yes. And here's how.

Go back to your picture of a cloud at the top symbolizing God and a stick figure at the bottom symbolizing you. Now draw a line from God to you, representing grace coming down, but before you end the line, curve it back up *through you* to God and put an arrow on the end. The grace goes back up. Grace comes down, goes through you, and back up to God.

It's a curved arrow.

We'll let it represent reciprocation.

All goodness starts from God, flows from him to us, flows through us, and back up to God. He is the Designer, Initiator, Motivator, and Worker of all good works. We are the vessels through which he operates. Get it? It's all grace.

And therefore it's all God's glory.

That's Paul's big idea: "It is God who works in you both to will and to do for His good pleasure" (Philippians 2:13).

Not only is the work all God's, but he's not stopping until it's done: "Being confident of this very thing, that He who has begun a good work in you will complete it until the day of Jesus Christ" (Philippians 1:6).

But it wouldn't be fair to the legalists if we didn't include the verse they most love to quote out of context (but don't miss Paul's big idea again at the end):

Therefore, my beloved, as you have always obeyed,
not as in my presence only, but now much more
in my absence, work out your own salvation with
fear and trembling; for it is God who works in
you both to will and to do for His good pleasure.
(Philippians 2:12–13)

Curved arrows. Ricochets. A reciprocation of God's beautiful initiative and grace. Loving him because he first loved you.

So, go forth and be holy. Do mighty deeds of valor for Jesus Christ. Slay giants. Subdue armies of darkness. Conquer your addictions and fears. Do missions. Or, if you prefer, be missional. Share the gospel. Win the lost. Feed the hungry. Serve the poor. Heal the wounds of a broken world in Jesus' name.

Be dedicated, consecrated, and sanctified.

But do it all with a humble consciousness of God's power doing the work.

Do it all while turning to Christ in moment-by-moment faith.

Do it all by the Holy Spirit, who makes all your blessings tangible.

And do it all with a thankful heart, grateful for the great privilege of being used by him.

Jesus said, "I am the vine, you are the branches. He who abides in Me, and I in him, bears much fruit; for without Me you can do nothing" (John 15:5).

Everyday faith in this simplest of truths is the secret of your sanctification.

CHAPTER 12

SECURITY

Neither sin, nor Satan, nor the world can put a Christian out his inheritance. Christ has already taken possession of it in their names and in their stead; and so it is secure to them. If weakness can overcome strength, impotency omnipotency, then may a Christian be kept out of his inheritance—but not until then.

THOMAS BROOKS (1600s)

You can't lose your salvation. Not even if you tried. Not even if you went out and invented a fat, juicy sin nobody has ever done before. Once you're saved, you're always saved. That teaching is called *eternal security*, and it is enormously scandalous.

It is also hugely controversial.

It shouldn't be. After all, what good is a salvation that doesn't save? What good is a rescue operation that throws the soggy sinner overboard in the end? Doesn't the thought of salvation lost make God the Great Ungifter? How can *eternal* life be a temporary possession? Is it conceivable that union with Christ, justification, propitiation, redemption, and the host of cosmic transformations collectively called salvation come with an OFF switch?

If the life you had with God can end, can you really call it eternal?

I'm predicting that no chapter in this book will generate more heat than this one. That's okay. If I'm going to dig my own grave, I'll dig it on the mountain of grace, and I'll happily go down lobbying for an efficacy in the Cross of Christ greater than mortals have dreamed.

What Is Eternal Security?

Here's a simple definition of eternal security: *God himself bears all the burden to keep you saved forever.* Your salvation is all of God: from him, by him, and for him. It is all of grace from beginning to end. As the burden was on his shoulders to save you, so it remains on his shoulders to keep you saved.

That's why we use the word *security.* You are secure in your relationship with the Father, the Son, and the Holy Spirit. You are secure in your forgiveness, your justification, your adoption, and your everlasting life. Like a priceless heirloom, you've been gently placed into God's most secure treasure house, there to be guarded forever.

Not all Christians agree on this doctrine. I'm a big fan of being charitable toward those of differing theological opinion. God loves people who disagree with me. I get that. Those who argue that a Christian can lose salvation are not my enemies; this is one of those areas where reasonable Christians disagree.

However, as I read Scripture, I find the evidence for eternal security woven so tightly into the doctrine of salvation that I just can't see how anyone can separate them.

So here are my top twelve reasons why you can't lose your salvation, resting on four attributes of the God of Almighty Shoulders: his grace, his power, his faithfulness, and his sovereignty. After these reasons I'll talk a little bit about a related teaching called the perseverance of the saints.

Secured by the Grace of God

1. Because all your sins are fully paid for, even the ones you're going to commit tomorrow.

When Jesus died on the cross, he didn't forget a single sin. It makes no difference when, on the timeline of your life, you actually commit those sins. Whether you commit them before you are saved or after doesn't matter. Jesus paid for *all* your sins—past, present, and future. He paid in full. God would damage his own honor if he were to punish you for a sin Christ already died for. How can that which has been washed away in the flood of Calvary love ever spoil your "so great a salvation" (Hebrews 2:3)? The Bible says that Jesus, after he had offered the one and only all-sufficient sacrifice to pay for all your sins, "sat down at the right hand of God" (Hebrews 10:12). Why? Because payment for your sins was utterly complete, meaning there is no conceivable circumstance under which you will ever pay for even one of them before God. (See also John 1:29; Romans 8:1; Hebrews 10:12; 1 John 2:1.)

2. Because your good works weren't required to get you saved, they can't be required to keep you saved.

When you think about it, there are basically two big reasons why God might kick you out of his family: too much sin or too little righteousness. We answered the first reason above, and here's the answer to the second. Good works—including religious observances, morality, and all your human blood, sweat, and tears piled on top it itself and then squared—is utterly excluded from the way of salvation. God saved you "not by works of righteousness" (Titus 3:5). Paul said, "Therefore by the deeds of the law no flesh will be justified in His sight" (Romans 3:20). There is no logic or Scripture under which good works can be a condition for continued salvation. Lewis Sperry Chafer observes, "A justification which is not subject to human merit could hardly be subject to human demerit."[70] (See also Zechariah 4:6; Ephesians 2:8–9; Titus 3:5.)

3. Because, as a Christian, you have been made a full partner in all that belongs to Christ. For God to unsave you, he would have to let go of Christ first.

Your union with Christ is the ultimate guarantee of your everlasting salvation. This beautiful gift sets Christianity in a league of its own. God does not bless you directly; he blesses Jesus Christ, and you are blessed in Christ. His provision *is* your provision. His power *is* your power. His holiness *is* your holiness. His security *is* your security. You have nothing apart from Christ and everything in him, forever. Scripture makes the remarkable claim that you have been made equal partners with the Son of God, and are included in all his rich blessings forevermore. "If children, then [you are] heirs—heirs of God and joint heirs with Christ" (Romans 8:17). You did not earn this privilege: God, in his marvelous grace, slathered it all over you.

For God to unsave you, he would have to either unravel the garment of union with Christ or let Christ fall from his throne. Not in a million eternities. The sparkling streams of amazing grace never will run dry. (See also Romans 8:16–17; Galatians 3:29, 4:7.)

Secured by the Power of God

4. Because your security is now in God's hands, not your own.

In the first moment you trusted Christ, your eternal destiny was eternally taken out of your hands. God took ownership of your future. He wrapped his hand around you, and he will never let you go. You are guarded by the omnipotence of God. He has more power in his little finger than the devil and all the hosts of darkness have combined. With one flex of his bicep, he can silence Satan's accusations, shatter hell's claims, still life's fiercest storms, subdue your heart's darkest passions, snap the chains of the world's allurements, and sweep your life's collected sins into the abyss of Calvary's all-sufficient blood. God is happily stuck with you. You have no say in the matter.

Let Christ's incredible promise sink deeply into your soul:

> *"My sheep hear My voice, and I know them, and*
> *they follow Me. And I give them eternal life,*
> *and they shall never perish; neither shall anyone*
> *snatch them out of My hand. My Father, who has*
> *given them to Me, is greater than all; and no one*
> *is able to snatch them out of My Father's hand."*
> *(John 10:27–29)*

5. Because salvation depends on God's ability, not yours.

All the biblical imagery of God as a shield, strong tower, and defender should squash the "conditional security" bug into a little gooey mess. If God is your "strong tower," name one power that's going to break through and drag you out of your saved position. Is he a strong tower or a strong*ish* tower? When Jude wrote God "is able," he used the Greek word *dunameo*, which means "he has the power." God has the power do what? "To keep you from stumbling, and to present you faultless before the presence of His glory with exceeding joy" (Jude 1:24).

The same omnipotent arm that spun innumerable stars into orbit and packed mind-numbing energy into every thimbleful of matter, the same Almighty hand that shattered the bars of death to raise Jesus from the tomb, the Lord God Omnipotent himself, has signed in blood an oath to preserve you for his heavenly Kingdom. You may fail ten thousand times, but God can do anything but fail. (See also Psalm 61:3; Proverbs 18:10; 2 Timothy 4:18.)

6. Because to unsave you, somebody would have to over-power God.

I'm a dad, and I would never let anybody hurt one of my kids. They'd have to kill me first. God adopted you into his family. He became your Father, and he takes that role with utmost seriousness. Peter explains that you are "kept" by the power of God forever (1 Peter 1:5). That word, translated "shielded" in some versions, means to post armed guards around someone. That's what God has done for you, only he's the arm and he's the guard. Who can defeat him? Sin can't. The devil can't. You can't. The demons can't. Your mistakes can't. Your addictions can't. Your rap sheet can't. Your in-laws can't. Your ex can't. And God won't. Consider yourself secured forever within the invincible arms of God. "Through faith

[you] are shielded by God's power until the coming of the salvation that is ready to be revealed in the last time" (1 Peter 1:5 NIV).

Secured by the Faithfulness of God

7. Because God promised to save you to the end, and he can't lie.

God is faithful—immeasurably more dependable than anyone else in your life. If he promises something, consider it done. If he starts something, consider it finished. When you blow it, he doesn't. When you turn faithless, he remains faithful. Not even the ages of eternity will witness the slightest flicker in the faithfulness of God, and therefore, in his secure grip on you. This is why Paul can say he is "confident of this very thing, that He who has begun a good work in you will complete it until the day of Jesus Christ" (Philippians 1:6).

His faithfulness is great. His mercies are new every morning. With God, there is no shadow of turning and no variation. He never works in fits and spurts, but like a mighty river, flows on and on in his own character.

For God to rescind your salvation, he would have to be unfaithful to himself, in which case he would cease being God, and this whole created order would have already folded in on itself in a moment of de-creation that would spoil Sunday dinner. Every time I screw up, I thank God he is faithful, and move on. (See also Ecclesiastes 3:14; 1 Corinthians 1:9; Philippians 1:6; Titus 1:2; Hebrews 6:18, 7:24–25; 10:14; James 1:17.)

8. Because God won't dump his children.

Most Christians have little clue of how enormous the

salvation package is. It's the biggest deal of all the big deals in your life. As part of the deal, God adopted you. You became his child in a special and intimate way. He became to you a loving, ideal Father. Even though you stray, you're still his kid. Even though you're a jerk, he's still your Father. Even through anything, he will not kick you out of his family.

God's faithfulness knows no bounds.

In the story of the prodigal son, even though the STD-risking, pierced, lice-ridden, loser of a son was far away from his father's house, he never stopped being his father's son. And so it is with you. You may fall under your Father's discipline, but that only proves his love (Hebrews 12:6). Christ himself issued the iron-clad guarantee that he "will by no means cast out" any who come to God by him (John 6:37). The Greek text uses a strong double negative: he "can't won't" reject you under any circumstance. (See also Luke 15:11–32; John 6:37; Romans 8:16; Hebrews 13:5.)

9. Because God won't withdraw his Spirit from you.

Never underestimate the jaw-dropping honor of being the Holy Spirit's home. God is with you, and God is for you, because God is in you. He has taken up permanent residence within your being. When you got saved, the Holy Spirit moved in. Paul describes the Spirit's presence as God's down payment on the full salvation package. He is the seal on the deal, the ink on the contract, and the earnest payment on all grace experiences yet to come. When it comes to your salvation, there's no going back. Not for you. Not for God. Not for anyone. Scripture says:

> *You also were included in Christ when you heard the message of truth, the gospel of your salvation.*

When you believed, you were marked in him with
a seal, the promised Holy Spirit, who is a deposit
guaranteeing our inheritance until the redemption
of those who are God's possession—to the praise of
his glory. (Ephesians 1:13–14 NIV)

Secured by the Sovereignty of God

10. Because your eternal future is already predetermined by God.

Whether you view salvation as a sovereign decision of election or a human decision of free will, there is no getting around the simple truth that once sinners step across the line of faith, their eternal destiny is sealed. It is taken from their control forever. Like strapping into a roller coaster, they're going for the whole ride because there are no exit ramps.

God has decreed your salvation to last forever, and so it shall. All the steps leading up to that moment were in his hand, and all the steps leading away from it to the ages of eternity are equally in his hand. Your destiny is so certain that God already calls your future glorification a done deal:

Whom He foreknew, He also predestined to be
conformed to the image of His Son, that He might
be the firstborn among many brethren. Moreover
whom He predestined, these He also called; whom
He called, these He also justified; and whom He
justified, these He also glorified. (Romans 8:29–30)

The decree of eternal salvation is eternally unalterable, and you can rest your soul in the hands of the sovereign Master and Commander of the universe. (See also Ephesians 1:4; 1 Peter 1:2; Revelation 13:8.)

11. Because God has willed your salvation to last until the end.

The word *end* in the Bible means something like a finish line (Greek, *telos*). What's the ultimate finish line for the Christian? Heaven. So, Scripture promises this: "[God] will also confirm you to the end, that you may be blameless in the day of our Lord Jesus Christ" (1 Corinthians 1:8). Who will confirm you till the end? You, by your strength? You, by your efforts? Your religion? Your activism? Your moral improvement? No. God alone does this, without one speck of help from you. He makes you stable and secure in your salvation, doing whatever it takes to keep you saved, until you reach your heavenly finish line. He will do this in such a way that when the penetrating gaze of the Almighty examines you, you will be found *blameless*. Not many people on earth would say that about you, but God does. This is the power of grace. By it, God has spoken decisively; he will not change his mind. (See also John 6:37; 1 Corinthians 1:8–9; 2 Timothy 1:12, 4:18; 1 Peter 1:5.)

12. Because God will overrule any being or power that tries to revoke your salvation.

Try to picture some foolish cadre forming an elaborate plot to kidnap you from the heavenly realms. They dress in camo, sneak up to heaven's gates—and immediately alarm bells begin to clang. Imagine the lightning bolts of wrath unleashed on them. Not even Satan can pry you from God's grip. People say that you should hold on to God, and that's good, I guess. But the real wonder is that he holds on to you. His grip won't slip, and nobody can snatch you out of his hand. No, not even you yourself on your very worst day.

I am persuaded that neither death nor life,
nor angels nor principalities nor powers,
nor things present nor things to come,
nor height nor depth, nor any other created thing,
shall be able to separate us from the love of God
which is in Christ Jesus our Lord.
(Romans 8:38–39)

Seriously Saved

The overwhelming testimony of Scripture is this: God himself bears all of the burden to get you saved, keep you saved, and bring you safely home at last. In the chain that connects you to heaven, not one link has been forged by your own might. Otherwise, you'd be doomed—for the whole chain would only be as strong as its weakest link.

Instead, in grace, God has set all your works aside. Salvation stands forever as his work, beginning, middle, and end. God is gracious, and therefore you are secure forever. God is omnipotent, and therefore you are secure forever. God is faithful, and therefore you are secure forever. God is sovereign, and therefore you are secure forever.

What more could you ask for?

A little voice inside you might hiss, *It's too good to be true.* That little Pharisee in your head, making you fret over your salvation, needs to shut up. That little Sadducee inside, convincing you to cower and grovel before your Maker, is telling you a lie. That little inner scribe, driving you to pray for salvation over and over again, is spouting the doctrines of demons; don't be a sucker.

Once saved, always saved.

That's how powerful Calvary is.

God's Integrity at Stake

There's an old preacher's story about a little old lady on her deathbed. Her novice pastor came to visit to make sure she was ready to go.

"Don't worry about me," she said, eyes gleaming and voice warbling. "I know the Lord is mine and I am his."

Her preacher gasped. Having been reared by a pack of howling legalists, he had no room in his theology for such breathtaking confidence. He tried to talk some humility into her.

"Yes, but God must judge you according to your deeds, and 'be sure your sins will find you out,' and—"

She shushed him.

"Young man," she said, "if I don't go to heaven when I die, then God will lose far more than I will lose."

The pastor sputtered with indignation. "What? Do you realize how arrogant—"

Again she interrupted him. "Listen, if I don't go to heaven, I will lose my soul forever, that's all. But if I don't go to heaven, God will lose his integrity. For he has promised to take to heaven all those who come to him by Christ, and that is how I have come."[71]

Can I get an amen?

Does this mean you can go out tomorrow and commit a sin and still go to heaven? The lawyer I live with is very concerned about this rhetorical question; she wants me to issue all kinds of caveats and warnings, but I won't. I will simply let grace stand there naked, and scandalous, and without qualifiers.

The answer is *yes*, with no *buts* in sight. Even if you could invent a new sin, you would never lose your salvation. It just doesn't depend on you. It all depends on Christ.

Whatever consequences for sin there may be in a Christian's life, you will never find dismissal from God's family among them.

Perseverance of the Saints

What about the perseverance of the saints? One of my favorite seminary professors, Dr. S. Lewis Johnson, defined this famous P in Calvinism's TULIP this way: "God secures in grace the salvation of true believers, keeping them from sinning as a practice, and preserving them from apostasy for life eternal. He preserves, we persevere as the result."[72]

The idea is that a genuine Christian can never sin in such a way as to lose salvation. God restrains us from such sin. Christians can't and don't continue in a lifestyle of sin, says this teaching. In fact, if you do sin so far as to fall away from Christ, or if you persist in a seriously sinful lifestyle, that is a sign that you were never saved to begin with. Louis Berkhof says, "It is, strictly speaking, not man but God who perseveres."[73]

The problem, however, happens when legalists use a doctrine that should be of great comfort to bash the Christian's confidence to pieces. Under this view it is nearly impossible for any human to say whether a person has finally fallen away until that person is dead. We can only view a person's life in snippets. We see cross-sections. To undercut salvation on the basis of failed perseverance is like sampling a half-baked cheesecake and declaring it mush.

Was Samson persevering in the faith when, after being anointed and filled by the Holy Spirit, he hopped into the land of pagan romance and fornication? If he had died before his hair grew back, would he have gone to hell?

What about David, the man after God's own heart? If he had died in bed with Bathsheba, would his low Perseverance Quotient have landed him in perdition?

Or Jacob, for deceiving Isaac? Or Moses for striking a rock that God had told him simply to speak to?

Would Peter have gone to hell if he had died the day after he denied Christ? Or Thomas, for denying the Resurrection? Can anyone say these people were "never saved to begin with"?

Perseverance of the saints has been misused to flog many a sensitive soul with duty and obligation and fear. "You'd better persevere in the faith *or else!*"

What should be a comfort has become a cudgel.

Even granting that salvation isn't just from the penalty of sin, but from the power of sin, too—which I believe—there is no way for any Christian to apply perseverance to anybody outside his or her own skin. I can't see your heart. I can never say whether or not your sin crosses a hypothesized point of no return.

I can't tell whether you're saved or not, at least not with infallible certitude. And I shouldn't try. Who am I to judge another's servant (Romans 14:4)? Did God die and appoint me fruit inspector?

If you tell me you have trusted in Christ and received him as your Savior, I will give you a big hug and welcome you to the family of God.

I go by your profession. God sees your heart.

Legalists will pit perseverance *against* eternal security, as if eternal security hands out a hall pass to sin, while perseverance of the saints doesn't.

Have a little faith. If the power of God *preserves* a Christian in such a way that a Christian *perseveres*, isn't that good news? Shouldn't those operations be automatic? Shouldn't we leave the results with God? The gospel doesn't summon people to perseverance, does it? The gospel's summons will ever be faith alone in Christ alone.

Shouldn't you be preaching all your perseverance sermons to God? Isn't that his burden, his responsibility? He's the one "who has begun a good work in you [and] will complete it until the day of Jesus Christ" (Philippians 1:6). Under grace, that's his job.

We must never let the fear of Christians behaving badly mar the simplicity and beauty of the gospel of grace. It is an epic mistake to mash the duties of perseverance into the free gospel of amazing grace.

You can't take yourself away from God. The devil can't take you away from God. Your pastor, priest, or pope can't take you away from God. God won't take you away from God. So what can separate you from God? Absolutely nothing.

You might feel shaky.

You might feel insecure and weak.

Regardless of your feelings, the fact is you are secure forever in the hands of your Father. Calvary love is all the guarantee you need.

If you were saved at the beginning of this year, you'll still be saved at the end of it. And a decade from now and a century from now you'll still be saved. And when the mountains crumble into the sea, and this old earth begins to dissolve, and our sun burns out its fuel and eternity rolls on, forever and evermore, you will still find yourself gripped by the grace and power of a God who loved you and gave himself for you.

The soul that on Jesus hath lean'd for repose.
I will not, I will not desert to his foes;
That soul, though all hell should endeavor to shake,
I'll never, no never, no never forsake.[74]

CHAPTER 13

ASSURANCE

Uncertainty as to our relationship with God is one of the
most enfeebling and dispiriting of things. It makes a man
heartless. It takes the pith out of him. He cannot fight;
he cannot run. He is easily dismayed and gives way.
He can do nothing for God. But when we know that we
are of God, we are vigorous, brave, invincible. There is
no more quickening truth than this of assurance.

HORATIUS BONAR (1800s)

I know I'm going to heaven. I know my sins are forgiven. I
know God loves me and lives inside me and I am his child.
I know these things, not because I am a better person than
anybody else, not because I am a pastor—paid to be holy—
and not because I am a charmingly good-looking Italian.

I know these things because the Bible tells me so, and I
have the priceless commodity known in theology as *assurance*.

Assurance is the flip side of eternal security's coin. Eternal
security is the Christian's objective reality; assurance is the
Christian's subjective confidence.

It might surprise you to know there is a giant theological pie-fight over assurance. Catholic theology since the Council of Trent argues, "A believer's assurance of pardon for his sins is a vain and ungodly confidence."[75] Of course, large swaths of non-Catholic Christianity—the groups that deny eternal security—would shout a big amen.

Our Reformed/Calvinist friends might warn against too much emphasis on assurance, working from the premise that continuance in a faithful lifestyle till death is the only assurance we can claim. John Murray writes, "Let us appreciate the doctrine of the perseverance of the saints and recognize that we may entertain the faith of our security in Christ only as we persevere in faith and holiness unto the end."[76]

I'm not so sure about that. I wonder how many earthly fathers would predicate their children's place in the family on obedience till the end?

Contrast this to Saint Augustine's more ancient assertion: "To be assured of our salvation is no arrogant stoutness. It is our faith. It is no pride; it is devotion. It is no presumption; it is God's promise."[77]

Scripture is clear: eternal life is not a "hope so" proposition; it is a "know so" proposition:

> *These things I have written to you who believe in the name of the Son of God, that you may know that you have eternal life, and that you may continue to believe in the name of the Son of God.*
> *(1 John 5:13)*

I'm not keeping my fingers crossed and hoping for the best. I'm resting in the finished work of Jesus Christ as my only hope; and if that's not enough, I've got no plan B. The biggest question of my life has been answered: I will spend eternity with God. No nagging doubts, no hellfire fears, and no heavenly frown threatens my peace with God. Though I am deeply conscious—and ever increasingly so—of my innate unworthiness, I am gripped by a hand of grace that I know will never let me go.

It wasn't always this way for me. Though I was saved as a kid, I was freaked out that it wouldn't stick. The buckshot of legalism punctured a thousand holes in my confidence. One phrase in particular worried me—it came from my Sunday school teacher more times than I could count. After describing something good that Christians should be doing, he would lean in and say, "If you're not doing [insert radical-type duty here], you'd better check your salvation experience!"

But I had a huge problem: having been saved very young, I couldn't remember my salvation experience. There was no experience for me to check. So I did what any self-respecting eight-, nine-, or ten-year-old would do: I prayed to receive Christ again. And again and again and again. I begged. I pleaded. I promised to try harder.

My doubts were not born of humility; they were the oozing scabs of Grace Deficit Disorder.

I knew the gospel outline, but it was so inconsistently intermingled with behavioral obligations that I never felt I'd done enough.

That anxiety slimed me like toxic mold. I prayed, read my Bible, shared my faith, knocked on doors to witness to strangers (oh, the humanity), played in my church worship band, never missed a prayer meeting, helped in Awana clubs, and helped with the youth group. All of this as a teenager.

And much of this out of an unresolved anxiety over God.

When I was seventeen, God flipped a switch for me and dropped the gift of assurance in my lap with such force that I've never looked back.

I was sitting in my cavernous high school gym in urban Chicago on a day when my gym teacher was absent. We were told to sit in the stands and do homework. I read a book. What I read blew my guilt-ridden, anxiety-induced, fear-driven, God-avoidant, damnation-brooding fretfulness out of the window once for all.

I got gracified. How?

By reading the first explanation of the Cross of Christ that really clicked for me.

Suddenly, God converted an echo-filled, stale gymnasium into a sanctuary. The noise of pickup basketball slipped into the background, and my eyes were opened to the finality of the Cross. In that moment, I knew I was saved. I knew my sins were gone. A weight had been lifted off my shoulders. My theological arrows turned around.

It wasn't the day of my salvation; I was quite conscious of that. It was the day of my assurance.

Christ really did pay my debt in full.

Christ really did die for me.

God really did love me.

I really could come to him "just as I am."

I really was saved.

My faith really did stick, the hour I first believed.

I really was a beloved member of the family of God all because of my Savior's blood.

I felt no pride, no presumption. Just a burden rolled away and a hope given wings. I have never seriously doubted my salvation since that day.

I've thought long and hard, over the years, wondering what made the difference. The truths I read that day were nothing new. I'd heard them in bits and pieces all my life. But something clicked for me. What was it? What was the secret of my assurance?

My assurance, just like everyone's, flows out of one proof and two evidences.

One Proof: The Word of God

I know beyond all doubt I am saved forever because the Bible tells me so. Jesus promised that whoever comes to God by him he will "by no means cast out" (John 6:37). I have come to God by him.

Christ's language is emphatic—a double negative in the original language, like a one-two punch in legalism's face. He will not hurl you out of his affections. He will not hurl you out of his arms. He will not hurl you out of his family. He will not hurl you out of the justification, redemption, propitiation, or salvation in which you stand. He will not hurl you out of his glorious, blood-bought church.

He promised.

What more proof do you need?

The title deed to your mansion in heaven has been signed in blood, sealed by the Spirit, and given to you in writing.

God invites you to come near "with a true heart in full assurance of faith" (Hebrews 10:22). This is the assurance birthed by Scripture integrated into your soul.

Paul prays for Christians to attain "to all the riches of the full assurance of understanding" (Colossians 2:2). This is the breathtaking confidence bubbling up from ever-deepening scriptural wells of grace in Jesus Christ.

The author of Hebrews desires that Christians "show the same diligence to the full assurance of hope until the end" (Hebrews 6:11). A promise from a God who cannot lie has to be the surest bet in life and death.

When God invites you to "come boldly to the throne of grace" he presumes a certain level of assurance (Hebrews 4:16). To step boldly before God? Really? That is nothing but a giant round peg in legalism's painfully tiny square hole.

On the day of Pentecost, three thousand people were saved. They were immediately added to the church and were baptized (Acts 2:41). Why the rush? Why not wait for fruit to develop? After all, shouldn't church leaders wave their Perseverance Geiger Counters over new converts' lives for a while to see if any holiness registers? Wouldn't that make more sense?

No.

Because salvation is as certain in that first hour as it will be in the ages of eternity. It is as certain for the Christian as the love of the Father is for the Son.

It is an immutable promise from an immutable God to a people he knows are embarrassingly mutable. That's why he draws a line, invites them to cross it, and then scoops them into his forever family the moment they do.

On your worst day, if you can scrape together the faith to do it, you can show the divine contract to the heavenly

Covenanter and insist he fulfill his end of the bargain.

And he will.

He loves that kind of audacious faith.

In fact, he'll fulfill his covenant whether you ask him to or not. Because God accomplishes his will on days when you don't care. What he promises, he does. What he starts, he finishes. You are not the point. Sorry. His own integrity is the point.

Jesus loves me, this I know,
For the Bible tells me so.

What more proof do I need?

None. That's why I offer only one proof and two evidences. The proof of Scripture stands external to the believer; the mega-pile of scriptural promises will never change. The subjective evidences, however, can change. They may buttress assurance, but in the final analysis, they don't prove it.

First Evidence:
The Inward Testimony of the Spirit

We are so damaged by the Fall that we need a little extra help in the confidence department. So, in addition to his Word, God graciously gives the brave assurance of his Spirit. The Holy Spirit whispers assurance over and over again into your soul: "The Spirit Himself bears witness with our spirit that we are children of God" (Romans 8:16).

Since before she could speak, I have told my (now teenage) daughter she is beautiful. Objectively speaking, she is; she's a knockout. I have a shotgun ready to handle the gorillas who plan to date her.

"Honey, you're beautiful," I say. I've said it ten thousand times, and it's true.

Does she think she's beautiful?

On good days, yes. On other days, not so much. It's fallen human nature—and especially adolescent nature—to doubt one's beauty or worth.

No matter how many times I say it, something has to happen inside her before it rings true, before the objective reality becomes subjective perception.

Enter the Holy Spirit. He is the master at worming our theology into our psychology. He helps make what is true about us become what we feel about ourselves. He does not do this in isolation from the Word—he always wields the Sword of the Word (Ephesians 6:17).

By that Word, the Spirit will compile Scripture truth into your soul (assuming you study it), so that one day it will suddenly click. This moment may feel like an epiphany, like it did for me on the day of my assurance. In reality, those weren't new truths for me; they were very old truths. They just never clicked like that before. Like Paul, the scales fell off my eyes and I could see (Acts 9:18).

When the Word is mixed with faith, the Spirit convinces us that we are children of God.

How else could Paul declare with such indomitable confidence, "I know whom I have believed and am persuaded that He is able to keep what I have committed to Him [i.e., my soul's safekeeping] until that Day" (2 Timothy 1:12). A lifetime of Bible study suddenly clicked for Paul as the Spirit compiled the grace operating system for him.

In the same way, I pray that the scales will fall from your eyes as well.

My old Sunday school teachers had a little country band. They'd gather around a gutbucket (look it up; it's a primitive bass guitar made from a steel bucket, a mop stick, and a length of twine, propped up by a hymnal) and sing:

> *My God is real,*
> *For I can feel*
> *Him in my soul.*

I can feel him, too. Not all the time. But sometimes he feels close and I know he's with me. It's not proof; it's evidence. If you want proof, look to the Word of God. If you want evidence, listen for the still, small voice of the Holy Spirit. He is always singing the tune of whatever Scripture you've learned to confirm your standing in grace.

Second Evidence: A Lifestyle of Growth and Holiness

Finally, we come to good works, as an effect, not a cause, of grace. As the fruit, not the root, of all God does in our lives. Jesus promised this fruit: "I am the vine, you are the branches. He who abides in Me, and I in him, bears much fruit" (John 15:5).

The produce aisle of God's work in your life includes both character and good works done God's way.

Character revolves around the fruit of the Spirit like Earth revolves around the sun (Galatians 5:22–23). This fruit—singular, not fruits—is Christ himself living in you. It is Christ's own love, joy, peace, and so on, flowing through you. As you grow in grace, you also grow in Christlikeness. Paul labored that "Christ be formed" among the Galatians (Galatians 4:19 KJV). Church leaders, he said, should equip Christians, that they might attain to the "measure of the stature of the fullness of Christ" (Ephesians 4:13).

There's not one molecule of goodness in your character that didn't require the supernatural machinery of heaven and the personal presence of Christ in you to produce, so there's no boasting.

When you see yourself as grace's biggest charity case, you're starting to get the picture.

Your good works are as much a function of grace as your character. Good works, done God's way, bubble up in the overflow of grace. Have you squeezed out a few good deeds this week? Helped any little old ladies across the street? Raked the leaves for an elderly neighbor? Brought fresh dough-nuts to your pastor on Sunday morning (no hint implied, I'm low carb)? Those works were "prepared beforehand" by God that you "should walk in them" (Ephesians 2:10). God planned them, God motivated them, God set the table for them, and God energized them. Who gets the praise?

To divorce good works from grace is to slaughter them. The Bible calls such deeds, however noble, "dead works" (Hebrews 6:1, 9:14).

Traditional legalists are nice enough to list the dead works they expect from you in the church bulletin, usually in the "ministry opportunity" section. Pitch in, and we'll all know you're saved.

Neo-legalists pluck at the heartstrings to rally participation in the latest good cause: clean water in a third-world nation, tutoring inner-city youth, Bible study at the wine bar—all potentially good works, but just as easily dead works when motivated by that pesky drive to conform.

All of which makes good works the least evidential of Christian evidences, and the riskiest ground of assurance.

It's just too easy to fake it, or to do this stuff in all sincerity but without the power of Christ:

> *"Many will say to Me in that day, 'Lord, Lord, have we not prophesied in Your name, cast out demons in Your name, and done many wonders in Your name?' And then I will declare to them, 'I never knew you; depart from Me, you who practice lawlessness!'"* (Matthew 7:22–23)

Good works have as much evidential value as circumcision. Was it possible for circumcision to be owned in a heartfelt way as a sign of a person's standing in grace? Definitely. It was equally possible that circumcision morphed into a badge of arrogant superiority or meaningless obligation.

It was in that context that Paul hammered the legalists who were infecting Galatia. *You know that rusty old knife that's so important to all of you circumcision inspectors?* he said, "I could wish that those who trouble you would even cut themselves off!" (Galatians 5:12).

Ouch.

Malfunction

Fruit—whether character or good works—does not guarantee spiritual life, but it does potentially indicate it. We're not tossing it out categorically; we're just setting it in its proper context.

What really frosts me, however, is hearing preachers bludgeon sensitive souls with the necessity of good works as a sign of faith. Again, shouldn't that be automatic? Is it fair to question a person's salvation because they're not up to your standards? Doesn't the God who sees the heart transform the heart, slowly, over time?

And even if some Christian jerk is using salvation to justify his or her sinful lifestyle, so what? Won't the Holy Spirit convict that person? Can't divine Providence yank the subsidies out of a sinning Christian's life? If they're not saved, doesn't their lie invalidate itself? Don't they know it? Who needs some caricature of a Westboro Baptist clone to wag the finger of shame?

If you know Christian friends who've jumped into sin, confront them in a spirit of gentleness, conscious of your own temptability (Galatians 6:1). Otherwise, let them alone.

Maybe they need to sink into the pig slop of life outside their Father's gates.

Watch how God brings them to their senses and back to grace.

God gives the grace of assurance to all who will receive it. Like any blessing of grace, it is offered freely, as part of salvation's inheritance, to anyone who takes God at his word. Assurance is offered to you, if you'll have it.

Faith.

But to cloud your heart with sin, to dull your spirit with selfishness and greed, or to neglect growth in grace is to invite uncertainty into your life.

I don't know your heart; that's between you and God.

I don't know what you've believed or not believed, received or not received. The early church baptized men and women upon their *profession* of faith; evidence would come later.

It isn't for me, or for you, to judge.

What is ours to embrace is the abiding promise of God, and his personal invitation to abide in Christ forever:

"I am the vine, you are the branches.
He who abides in Me, and I in him, bears much fruit;
for without Me you can do nothing." (John 15:5)

CHAPTER 14

LIBERTY

Only what God has commanded in His Word should be
regarded as binding; in all else there may be liberty of actions.
JOHN OWEN (1700s)

Gracification brings Christians to a special place of freedom.
God says, "Do what you want."

Really.

Follow your heart. Pursue your dreams. Captain your ship.
Do what you want. Don't let fear of other people's opinions
suck the life out of you. Ditch the rules. Fly, little bird. Be free.

*John 8:32: "And you shall know the truth, and the truth shall
make you free."*

*Galatians 5:1: Stand fast therefore in the liberty by which
Christ has made us free, and do not be entangled again with a
yoke of bondage.*

Becoming a Christian does not mean swapping the bad

prison of sin for the "good prison" of religion. God sets you on a vast plain of radical grace, with no fences in sight, and says, "Be free."

Before I came to my present church in California, I went through the interview process at a church in another state. The interview went swimmingly until the topic of drinking came up. They asked if I considered drinking a sin.

You have to know something about me: Having grown up fundamentalist, my lifetime consumption of alcoholic beverages could fit in a Venti-sized Starbucks cup, and much of that was from Nyquil. I never acquired a taste for booze, even though my truck-driving dad—who sent me to church and waited outside reading a paper and enjoying a good smoke—moonlighted as a longtime bartender. However, I've come to believe what I told those good Baptist board members: The Bible does not prohibit responsible and moderate consumption of alcoholic beverages by adults. Drunkenness is a sin; drinking is not.

Most of the board members seemed okay with that, but there was one corner of the room where dark clouds formed. I saw the eyebrows go up, the eyes widen, the fist clench on the table.

"If you were at a wedding, would you drink champagne?" he asked.

"Yes," I said.

"Even if there were young people present?"

"Yes. It's a wedding. It's a toast. It's kind of rude not to participate."

"Well, I don't want my teenage son seeing his pastor drink," he said.

I said, "Do you have a written policy against drinking?"

"Well, no."

"So, let me get this right: as your pastor, I'd get in trouble with you for participating in a biblically permissible activity that is also not prohibited by any written policy of the church—I'd get in trouble if I did that? Is that what you're saying?"

Crickets.

I pressed on. "So, it's kind of like bumping into the invisible wall. There are unspoken rules you expect your pastor to follow, and I wouldn't know about them until it's too late."

Blushes. A few head nods.

"Do you see how creepy it would feel to live like that? I'd always be on edge. Can you understand that?"

"I guess."

"Besides, I want our teenagers to understand there are things I can do that they can't do. I can drive a car. I can hold a woman's hand and kiss her in public, go into a house with her, shut the door, turn off the lights, and hop in bed with her— so long as she's my wife. I have adult privileges they don't have. I have marital privileges they don't have. That's what I want our teenagers to understand."

They offered me the job.

But I went elsewhere. I will never again place my life in a setting permeated by legalism. And I certainly won't raise my kids in that environment.

Christian liberty is the birthright of every child of God. There will always be legalists pecking away at your freedom. Don't let them. Push them back. Exit the premises if you have to.

Within the parameters established by God's written Word, you are free.

Don't let pharisaical traditions squeeze the life out of you.

What about the Weaker Brother?

There is nothing in the Bible against offending the tastes of a brother or sister in Christ. You get to offend them. Be free.

You cannot, however, cause a *weaker* Christian to stumble. It surprises me how often, in discussions of Christian liberty, preachers who ought to know better forget the word *weaker*.

Scripture affirms, "But beware lest somehow this liberty of yours become a stumbling block [Greek: *skandalon*] to those who are weak" (1 Corinthians 8:9).

In the context, Paul is talking about meat that has been ritually offered to idols before hitting the butcher's meat case. For Christians, he says, an idol is nothing, so it's no big deal to eat that meat. But for freshly converted pagans, idols were everything. Idols were the dominant force in their lives. And meat that had been offered to an idol presented a powerful pull back into paganism.

So don't serve that meat to them. Don't buy that meat in front of them. Don't wave that sizzling rib-eye, formerly known as an offering to an idol, under their noses.

That's the idea.

They're weaker. Their old gods still tug at their heartstrings. Don't needlessly tempt them. Don't put a skandalon in their path—a snare that would cause them to stumble.

It is all-important to define the weaker Christian with

crystal clarity: a weaker Christian is a novice Christian who will be strongly tempted to do what they see you doing, to their own spiritual harm. It's not enough that a fellow Christian disapproves of your actions; that doesn't necessarily make them weaker.

Even if the idol is nothing, to those who are young in the faith it is a substitute god; don't tempt them. "If anyone sees you who have knowledge eating in an idol's temple, will not the conscience of him who is weak be emboldened to eat those things offered to idols?" (1 Corinthians 8:10).

Three qualifiers define the weaker Christian: (1) they are novices to the faith; (2) they are tempted to do the thing you're doing; and (3) it's to their own detriment and harm. In other words, they are weaker.

Yield.

But do not for a moment yield to those who claim to be stronger.

That's the point.

Innumerable legalists have pounded the hammer of "giving offense" on the head of Christian liberty. They are the ones offended. They are the ones crushing the freedom out of you. They are the self-appointed guardians of morality. They are anything but *weaker*.

As a twenty-something youth pastor, I was summoned to appear at a special board meeting called to take up a case against me in relation to the unpardonable sin: I went dancing. It was a square dance, and my date was my mother, in honor of her birthday, but I did the deed, and the board called me to account.

We had no official policy against dancing, so I never agreed to the deal.

Nobody in my church or youth group attended the dance to be tempted by my sultry moves.

All that mattered was the whisper mill hissing over rumors of my dancing.

I wish I'd had the guts back then to ask the board members if my dancing tempted them to dance. To ask if my dancing caused them to stumble. To find out if they were weaker brothers or not. Because if they weren't weaker brothers, *they had nothing to say to me.*

But I was only twenty-something, and they were all over a hundred, and they intimidated me.

Can you see how I come by my hatred of legalism honestly?

The simple fact is that no weaker Christians were harmed by my dancing.

I once had an elderly man in one of my churches—a pillar of faith, famous for preaching, by then retired—approach me out of the blue with this loving tidbit of grace: "Pastor, if this church ever has a dance, I'm walking out that door and never coming back."

Okay then.

Why is it that the only ones taking offense are supposedly stronger Christians who've been at it a lot longer than the rest of us? The very ones who would never think of doing the proposed activity, yet they play the "weaker brother" card as if it's a sin to offend their scruples?

The next time some smug fault finders whack you with the "you're causing offense" fly-swatter, whack them back with a combination of devastating punches:

Does the Bible explicitly prohibit the activity? Where?

Are you a new, baby Christian?

Are you tempted to do this same activity?

Will it harm your spirit if you do?

At the second *no*, the conversation should be over. (I'm assuming a *no* for the first question; if the Bible explicitly prohibits the activity, that's a different story.) Don't let the legalists control you. Don't let their rules constrict you. Don't fall into their self-limiting trap. Don't even get into an argument. All you have to say is, "The only offensive thing here is your legalism. Have a nice day." To the veteran weaker Christian who ought to have moved past these things, all we can say is, "*Grow up.*"

Let no one judge you in food or in drink, or regarding
a festival or a new moon or sabbaths, which are a
shadow of things to come, but the substance is of Christ.
(Colossians 2:16–17)

I can regale you with appalling stories of Christians judging Christians over dancing, drinking, card playing, movies, rock music, smoking, church on Saturday, the Lord's Supper, women in makeup, women in pants, not wearing a hat, not dressing up for church, women in head coverings, using antidepressants, and going into sports bars—stories in which legalists anoint themselves as champions of a hypothetical weaker brother or sister so that they might trample your liberty in Christ.

Thank God for grace.

The genuinely weaker Christian will come with a spirit

of timidity, worried about falling into temptation. The Bible says they will be "grieved" (Romans 14:15). They will be legitimately saddened. When you see that, yield. Don't do the deed. Sacrifice your rights. Put away the wine and drink Pepsi. Never let your choices put a stumbling block in the way of a novice Christian who is taking faltering baby steps on the way to growth. Tune your heart to self-sacrifice to meet a rookie Christian's needs.

But those who are not timid or tempted are also not weak. They're control freaks. They're bullies who, by now, ought to know better. Don't yield. The Bible tells you not to:

> *This occurred because of false brethren secretly brought in (who came in by stealth to spy out our liberty which we have in Christ Jesus, that they might bring us into bondage), to whom we did not yield submission even for an hour, that the truth of the gospel might continue with you. (Galatians 2:4–5)*

The truth of the gospel is at stake. Jesus did not shed his redeeming blood so that pucker-faced killjoys could yank your chain. The gospel of grace will not long endure where legalists get their way. Stand firm. Let them sputter and fume all they want. Be free.

The Myth of the Hypothesized Observer

One last dirty trick bears mentioning: the trick of the "hypothesized observer."

What if there's a genuine weaker brother on the other side of the restaurant who sees you order wine with your dinner? Wouldn't that tempt him? Better safe than sorry.

Ugh.

If that's the rule we must follow, don't do anything.

Really. Sit in a chair, and don't even turn on the TV. Maybe you can rock, but be sure not to roll. Better yet, don't move a muscle. And don't have a thought. Because *everything* offends *somebody*, so just freeze and wait for heaven.

I talked to a therapist friend who had a client with a shoe fetish, and shoes were his temptation, so. . .

Forget it.

The hypothesized observer must be genuinely weaker and visible, or at least highly likely. Given those conditions, Romans 15:1 applies: "We then who are strong ought to bear with the scruples of the weak, and not to please ourselves." Grace yields. Cancel the wine. Skip the dance. Use your gracified common sense on a case-by-case basis, and don't get sucked into the vortex of rules. The same applies if you know someone is susceptible to temptation and they are at or near your table.

But that would make them the opposite of hypothesized, wouldn't it?

Offending a fellow Christian isn't the standard; tempting a *weaker* Christian is. The weaker brother or sister has an obligation to speak up, so be free until that happens. Don't even ask if everybody's okay with what you'd like to do (1 Corinthians 10:27). Listen to the Bible and have fun.

On the flip side, you need to come to grips with this less-than-pleasant truth: other Christians are free to offend *you*.

What you like or don't like isn't their problem. They may sip wine coolers. They may dance. They may disco dance. They may even play shuffleboard. Or poker. Or get the queen of hearts tattooed on their forearms while grooving to disco at a poker tournament. Your scowl of dissatisfaction sets you on the precipice of legalism's slippery slope. "Who are you to judge another's servant?" (Romans 14:4).

If you feel tempted and weak, speak up. Otherwise, celebrate their tattoos and show others the grace you'd like them to show you.

Christ's death shattered prison bars. The stupendous fact of redemption means you are nobody's slave and nobody's master. Never yield to tyranny—not to Satan, not to sin, not to legalism, and most certainly not to the tyranny of crotchety old Bible-thumping prunes.

The Savior who redeemed you through his death on Calvary's hill wasn't joking when he said the truth will make you free.

Follow Your Heart

Your birthright lifts you into "the glorious liberty of the children of God" (Romans 8:21). Christ set the captives free.

Why cower before the bun-topped church lady's icy gaze?

Why yield to the disapproving shake of the crabby elder's head?

Why cringe before the neo-legalist's blanket insistence on vows of near poverty or third-world mission trips? God has told nobody his will for your life except you.

And he *has* told you. First in Scripture, and then deep inside, in the quiet longings of your gracified heart.

When your heart is good and gracified, it becomes a reliable guide for you. Follow your heart. Do what you want— do what the deepest and best part of you really wants. Within the expansive plains of grace, chase after your dreams.

Be free. Truly free. Free from internal bonds of addiction and fear. Free from external constraints of judgmental morons. Free from harsh parents hissing from their graves. Free from other people's opinions. Free from all the insanity of your imbecilic family tree. Free from the wreck you've made of your past. Free from habits that spoil your joy.

You died to all those things. Reckon yourself dead to them.

And then walk in newness of life.

Shake off those unlocked shackles, and by the power of Christ within you, and with the promises of grace before you, chart a destiny as big as the life you hoped you could live but never dared to.

Faith is the victory.

Grace is the glory.

A life of faith, rooted in grace, simply cannot lose.

CHAPTER 15

GLORY

Someday you will read in the papers that D. L. Moody of East Northfield is dead. Don't you believe a word of it! At that moment I shall be more alive than I am now; I shall have gone up higher, that is all, out of this old clay tenement into a house that is immortal—a body that death cannot touch, that sin cannot taint; a body fashioned like unto His glorious body.

D. L. MOODY (1800s)

God is glorified by what he does for you, not by what you do for him. His glory lies hidden in his grace. It's a shocker for most Christians, but your good works do not glorify God. How can they? If glory rightly goes to the doer of the deed, then you're the one who should receive the praise. The good works you do are done to your own glory.

So go ahead and boast.

But the good works that Christ does count for his glory.

I hear the objections already: What about Matthew 5:16? Jesus said, "Let your light so shine before men, that they may see your good works and glorify your Father in heaven."

Doesn't that prove our good works glorify God?

No.

It is *people* who glorify God—lost people, who are looking at you. They are the "they" in this verse.

Let your light shine, Jesus said.

What light?

Christ's own radiant glory dwelling in you. He dazzles all who behold him. Even the angels bow before his glory. And as he sanctifies you, his light shines through you more and more. Your good works are nothing but the bubbling over of God's grace. They are God's works through you. God's glory on display.

Jesus brought that glory with him when he moved inside you. He is constructing within you a shimmering edifice of grace. Grace thinking. Grace believing. Grace instinct. He welds together an interlocking structure of truth with truth, and no icy blast of legalism can shake it.

God is glorified by what he does for you, not by what you do for him.

My great passion and hope for you today, and for the church at large, is that we might recapture this simple wonder taught throughout Scripture: the glory of God is his grace.

Not what you do for him (works).

But what he does for you (grace).

God loves to bless you. He loves to provide for you. He loves to clean up after you. He never gripes. Never moans about what a wreck you are. He rolls up his sleeves and makes all things new.

Your sins won't deter him.

Your faithlessness won't depress him.

Your fickleness won't demoralize him.

Your frailties won't dishearten him.

Your tantrums won't daunt him.

God is eternally satisfied with you. It is God's great delight to bless you better than you deserve. He is not grudging. He is not sparing. He is not cheap.

Every day, the voice of grace cries out to you, "He who did not spare His own Son, but delivered Him up for us all, how shall He not with Him also freely give us all things?" (Romans 8:32).

The angels bow in adoration and praise at God's boundless grace for you.

The demons spit and fume that God should love you so well.

The devil roars. The gates of hell quaver. The starry universe itself stands on tiptoe, in eager anticipation of that marvelous day when the grace of God will explode in a fireworks show to dazzle the cosmos forever.

> *The earnest expectation of the creation eagerly*
> *waits for the revealing of the sons of God. . . .*
> *Because the creation itself also will be delivered*
> *from the bondage of corruption into the glorious*
> *liberty of the children of God. (Romans 8:19, 21)*

Grace will be the glorious theme of saints and angels for all the ages long.

It must become, therefore, the great theme of the church today. When grace fills our hearts, God's glory fills our world.

Isn't that what we need?

Isn't that what we want?

God is glorified by what he does for you, not by what you do for him.

Until you understand that, you don't understand your mission on planet Earth. You don't really understand the reason for your existence: humankind's "chief end is to glorify God and to enjoy him forever," said the Pilgrims' generation. I say, "Amen."

How will you do that? Through strivings? Sacrifices? Doing your duty? Giving your all? Grace Deficit Disorder on steroids?

Or through the unspeakable riches of grace?

How else can you "enjoy him forever"?

On the basis of the Word of God, I hereby set you free from trying to glorify God by your own good deeds. Give it up. Rest. Cease striving. Be still and know that he is God. Sit down, Martha. Stand still, Moses. Take a nap, Elijah. Fear not, disciple. At ease, soldier.

When legalism sucks the grace out of the room, it sucks the glory out, too.

Because God is glorified not by what you do for him, but by what he does for you.

You exist for "the praise of the glory of his grace" (Ephesians 1:6).

His glory is hidden in his grace.

The psalmist sings, "Not unto us, O LORD, not unto us, but unto thy name give glory, for thy mercy [literally, *grace*], and for thy truth's sake" (Psalm 115:1 KJV).

When God serves, when God blesses, when God gives, when God provides, when God loves, when God forgives, when God acts, when God saves, when God keeps, then God is to be praised. Then the angels pop the corks on heaven's champagne and the party begins in earnest. God's glory is his grace.

He is glorified by what he does for you, not by what you do for him.

So what does this mean for you if you want to glorify him more?

Position Yourself

If God's glory is in his grace, and if you desire to bring maximum glory to God in this lifetime and the next, what should you do?

It's simple, really.

Tune your heart to grace.

Teach your spirit to resonate to heaven's harmonic frequency. How?

Make a big deal of the Cross of Christ. The Cross has endless power to recalibrate your soul to grace. Return to it over and over and over again. All through life, until death, keep coming back to the Cross. Delve into its meaning. Embrace its rich vocabulary. Speak the blood-accented language of the heavenly realms.

Learn your riches in Christ. Step into your inheritance. Understand the priceless portfolio that became yours the day you received Christ. Claim it. Believe it. Rise up to your high calling. Shed the legalistic skin and wrap yourself in a God of all grace.

Give yourself permission to be yourself. In grace, God accepts you exactly as you are. Now you do the same. The crud in your life has to go, but it has already gone in reality, and will go in habit, as you tune your heart to grace. You possess a unique combination of gifts and dreams, experiences and passions. Nobody is quite like you. Nobody can bless the world as you can. You don't need to try to be like anybody else. Grace invites you to be yourself. And to say, *"By the grace of God, I am what I am"* (1 Corinthians 15:10).

Next, extend that same permission to others. Die to the irresistible urge to edit other people. Unless harm might come, let them be themselves. Don't fix. Don't fuss. Don't correct all the time. Just as grace accepted you—just as you are—so accept others. Be okay with God's pace for them, especially if they're close to you. If they will be graceless, then you be grace-full. You be the one who models grace for your family, your workplace, your world. Humbly. Patiently. Persistently. Lovingly. Let grace shine its light, and even a child will see.

Always watch the arrows. Is the flow, as you see it, from God to you, or the other way around? Learn legalism's dissonance. Be sensitive to that death-dealing screech. Turn it off when you hear it, if you can. Or else, tune it out. Repudiate it. Reverse direction. Don't let it in. Have no patience for it in your life.

Always have compassion on the graceless in the world. On those without life's essentials, to be sure. But on those without heaven's essentials, above all. May your heart beat with compassion for earth's walking dead, and may your lips and life ever be ready to tell the story of Jesus.

Tune your heart to grace. Study it. Learn it. Sing it. Speak it. Show it. Hear it. Befriend it. Love it. Because the greater the pipeline of grace flowing from God to you, the greater the fireworks of glory flowing from you to God.

Our intervention is over. Our GDD has been dragged out of hiding. Our legalism, whether traditional or neo, has been confronted. The healing streams of grace have been opened. Let's fold up the chairs. Pitch the Styrofoam coffee cups. It's time to move on. It's time to move forward. It's time to live the gracified life.

I pray that wherever you may go, and whatever paths God may lead you down, you will be found resting in the grace of a God who delights in you. I can't wait to meet you in heaven and to embrace you as a friend who's been forgiven, healed, filled up, and sent out by the matchless grace of God.

 Heaven

The entire grace enterprise of God has but one grand objective: "That in the ages to come He might show the exceeding riches of His grace in His kindness toward us in Christ Jesus" (Ephesians 2:7).

Eternal glory shines more brightly because God forgave a wreck like me.

The angelic roar is louder, the celestial happiness greater, and the Father's smile brighter because I am there, in heaven, seated at my Savior's side. Undeserving as I am, and unworthy as I know myself to be, I've been made worthy. I've been qualified for endless kindness from God's generous hand.

So you can expect me to be standing tall before God's

throne, "to the praise of the glory of his grace" (Ephesians 1:6).

What a moment that will be when the gaze of heaven locks onto Jesus. All things, great and small, will bow before him.

A spontaneous outburst of praise will ring through heaven's halls as God the Father crowns Jesus Christ Lord of All. What glory! What great joy! Thanksgiving will burst from our hearts. Adoration will gush from our lips. With our whole selves, the redeemed of the Lord will glorify the great name of our Savior and Lord. The creation itself will join the song. And Christ's greatest glory will always be his beautiful, blood-bought grace, most resplendent in a former wretch like me.

EPILOGUE:
THE ALPHABET OF GRACE

I love the acronym for grace, God's Riches At Christ's Expense. As true as it is, it's just not enough. The vastness of grace needs a little more, so let's revel in the alphabet of God's grace.

A. God's grace is AMAZING. Words can't define it. Minds can't contain it. Hearts can't explain it.

B. His grace is BOUNTIFUL. It overflows and bubbles over, and is never sparing or cheap.

C. Such grace is COSTLY. For God demonstrated his unfathomable love for us, in that Christ died for our sins.

D. God's grace is DETERMINED. Though I push him away, he still pushes back with kindness, forgiveness, and love.

E. His grace is EVERLASTING. From the counsels of ages past, to the glories of eternity future, his grace never waxes or wanes or shows signs of age.

F. God's grace is FREE. There are no strings attached, and he doesn't want us to pay him back. It's unconditional. Undeserved. Unrecompensed. Unmatched.

G. His grace is GLORIOUS. The blinding brilliance of divine grace for lost sinners will so dazzle the saints and angels that they will raise a cheer to echo through heaven's halls forever.

H. God's grace is HOLY. He couldn't make war in his own character to make peace with us, so he washed us in the blood of Jesus and made us white as snow.

I. His grace is INTIMATE. He knows us by name, and leans into our faintest whispers. He wants our company more than we can know.

J. God's grace is JESUS, casting down his royal crown, stripping off his glorious robe and covering over his radiant beams. God's grace is JESUS, coming to earth in a virgin's womb. JESUS friend of sinners, sweating great drops of blood. JESUS in his unjust trials, beaten and bloodied, but unbowed. God's grace is JESUS CHRIST, the spotless Lamb of God nailed to an old rugged cross, where the dearest and best, for a world of lost sinners was slain.

K. His grace is KIND. Gentle shepherd, come and feed us, for we need your help to find our way.

L. The grace of God is LOYAL. He will never desert us or forsake us.

M. The grace of God is MAGNANIMOUS. He is generous beyond measure, and lavishes on us riches beyond compare.

N. His grace is NEW EVERY MORNING. We can't wear it out, and the needle never points to empty.

O. The grace of God OVERFLOWS. Super-abounding to the chief of sinners.

P. His grace PROVIDES all our needs, according to his riches in Christ Jesus.

Q. God's grace never QUITS. It's not our grasp of God; it's his grasp of us that matters most.

R. God's grace RESTORES to us the years the locusts have eaten; for *only God can* turn back the clock on our dumb mistakes.

S. God's grace is a SAVING grace. It makes us a new creation, with a new name, and a status fit for royalty.

T. His grace is TRIUMPHANT. He towers over the world, the flesh, the devil, and all our sins and shame. In all these things, we are more than conquerors through Christ who loved us.

U. God's grace is UNDESERVED. God loves us because of who and what he is, never because of who and what we are or what we have done or haven't done.

V. God's grace is VAST. It is broader than the scope of our transgressions, far greater than all our sin and shame.

W. His grace is WONDERFUL. O for a thousand tongues to sing my great Redeemer's praise, the glories of my God and King, the triumphs of His grace.

X. His grace is eXCEPTIONAL. There's nothing like it. Nothing beside it. There is no God like our God. There is no grace like his grace.

Y. God's grace YEARNS for us to know him and to plumb the depths of his matchless love.

Z. His grace is the ZENITH of all our hopes and all our dreams, and more than we could ask or think. When all life's trials are over, and when the new creation comes, amazing grace will fill heaven's halls for all the ages long.

Thanks be to God for his unspeakable gift.

QUESTIONS FOR DISCUSSION
AND REFLECTION

Chapter 1: Terms

1. Do you have your own working definition of *grace*? What is it?

2. Which kind of legalism has been predominant in your understanding of Christianity—neo-legalism or traditional legalism?

3. How would you feel if your preacher or Bible teacher went for a couple of months without telling you to do something?

4. What does Hebrews 13:9 say about grace?

Chapter 2: Overload

1. What Christian clichés have you heard? When you really think about them, do they mean anything?

2. In your experience, how focused has the language of the gospel been on the Cross of Christ?

3. Have you ever noticed Grace Deficit Disorder in your own life? How has it manifested?

4. What does Galatians 1:6–9 imply about the dangers of GDD?

Chapter 3: Lordship

1. What do you know about what has been called the lordship controversy? What is your understanding of the term "cheap grace"?

2. Have you ever struggled to put the freeness and costliness of grace together? Where have you landed in that struggle?

3. How scandalous does grace seem to you?

4. What do Isaiah 55:1–2; John 19:30; Romans 3:24; and Revelation 22:17 suggest about the cost of salvation?

Chapter 4: Neo-Mishnah

1. What extra-biblical rules affect your circle of friends?

2. Do you know anybody who just can't fit in to your church's Christian culture, no matter how hard they try? How have you responded to them?

3. Can you see how your need for peer approval affects your life with God?

4. What does Colossians 2:8 tell you about following extra-biblical rules and teachings?

Chapter 5: The Gap

1. Have you heard the teaching that the God of the Old Testament and God of the New Testament are different? What do you think about that?

2. Do you have more trouble imagining the holiness of God or the love of God? Why do you think that is?

3. In what ways is a healthy doctrine of grace dependent on a high view of the holiness of God?

4. What does Isaiah 55:8–9 say about God's exalted status?

Chapter 6: Worldliness

1. What comes to mind when you hear the word *worldliness*?

2. How does worldliness show up among the Christians you know?

3. How is worldliness a manifestation of GDD?

4. What do think Jesus means in John 15:18–19 when he talks about the world hating Christians?

Chapter 7: Shallow

1. Has God placed any truly wise people in your life? What impact have they had on you?

2. Describe a time when your gut instincts told you something before your mind could put words to it.

3. What role should Bible study and theology play in the average Christian's life?

4. What does Philippians 2:5 say about the mind of Christ?

Chapter 8: Fuel

1. Have you ever thought about why you—or anybody—should serve God? What conclusions have you come to?

2. Judging by your church experiences, what do you think motivates most Christian service in our land today?

3. Which of Michael Green's motivations resonates most with you? Why?

4. What does Romans 5:5 say about our spiritual fuel?

Chapter 9: Bouncers

1. Have you ever felt like you didn't belong in a certain church? What made you feel that way?

2. Have you ever thought a certain person didn't belong in your church? Or your kids' youth group? Why?

3. Describe a time when you've seen a Jonah or an "elder brother" in action.

4. What does Luke 14:21 indicate about the people to whom God extends grace?

Chapter 10: The Cross

1. What comes to your mind and emotions when you think of the Cross?

2. How does the Messianic Secret help make sense of Christ's ministry?

3. How familiar are you with the theological terms in this chapter? Do any jump out at you or have special meaning for you?

4. What does 1 Corinthians 2:2 tell you about the centrality of the Cross?

Chapter 11: Sanctification

1. Which of sanctification's four "planks" resonates most with you? Do any seem weird or even wrong? Why?
2. Have your efforts to be holy worn you out? Feel more like Martha in the kitchen than Mary in the living room with Jesus? What changes can you make?
3. How does the idea of sanctification by grace sit with you?
4. How might Colossians 2:6 support sanctification by grace?

Chapter 12: Security

1. Have you ever heard of eternal security? Has it been portrayed positively or negatively?
2. Which of the twelve reasons do you struggle with most? Why?
3. Which reasons are most powerful for you? Amazing? Meaningful? Why?
4. What does Hebrews 13:5 say about your security in Christ?

Chapter 13: Assurance

1. How confident are you of your salvation? Is it okay to be confident?

2. Why do you think this chapter offers one proof and two evidences? What's the difference between evidence and proof? Why not just call them all proofs?

3. Has anyone ever perceived your assurance with arrogance? How did you handle that?

4. How might Romans 8:31 contribute to your sense of assurance?

Chapter 14: Liberty

1. What extra-biblical rules do you (or others you might know) associate with Christianity? What do you think about those rules?

2. Have you ever been slimed with the "weaker brother" argument from a veteran legalist? How did that go for you?

3. Does the idea of following your heart feel scandalous to you? What would Jesus say?

4. What can you learn from Psalm 37:4 about your heart's deepest desires?

Chapter 15: Glory

1. How does the assertion that God is glorified by his grace sit with you? What are your thoughts?

2. How often do you think most Christians think about or care about the glory of God? How high is it on your radar?

3. How might confidence of heaven affect your life on earth? How might the idea of heavenly reward affect your life on earth?

4. What does Colossians 3:1–4 say about a heaven-centric mind-set?

ENDNOTES

1. Ray C. Stedman, "Legalism," www.raystedman.org/thematic-studies/new-covenant/legalism.

2. Harry Ironside, "What Is the Gospel?" http://remnantradio.org/Mirror/www.jesus-is-savior.com/BTP/Dr_Harry_Ironside/what_is_the_gospel.htm.

3. *A Thief in the Night*, Mark 4 Pictures, 1972. Quote is from scene that begins at 8:41; http://www.youtube.com/watch?v=QnsXGkx4FWU.

4. Thanks to Robert Farrar Capon for this perspective, in *The Parables of Grace* (Grand Rapids, MI: Eerdmans, 1988), 158–59.

5. Ironside, "What Is the Gospel?"

6. Josephus Flavius, "Discourse to the Greeks Concerning Hades," in *Josephus: The Complete Works*, trans. William Whiston (Nashville, TN: Thomas Nelson, 1998), 976. The authorship of this tract is under dispute. But whether it was composed by Josephus, Hippolytus, or another ancient leader, it nonetheless displays the kind of legalism that has tormented God's people since the beginning.

7. In case you don't recognize it, this phrase is from the song "Oh, Rock My Soul," by Peter Yarrow (1964), which was a popular campfire song when I was growing up.

8. John R. W. Stott and Everett F. Harrison, "Must Christ Be Lord to Be Saviour?" *Eternity* 10 (Sept. 1959): 14–18, 36–37, 48.

9. Thomas G. Lewellen outlines some of this history in "Has Lordship Salvation Been Taught throughout Church History?" in *Bibliotheca Sacra* 147, no. 585 (Jan. 1990): 54–68. Starting with Augustine and on through Luther and Calvin, Lewellen traces a more passive idea of faith, demonstrating how it was the English Puritans who added the more active

component of obedience as faith's necessary sign. This view, enshrined in the Westminster Confession, guides many lordship advocates today.

10. These lists are based on my own perceptions of each author's body of work.

11. John MacArthur, *The Gospel According to Jesus* (Grand Rapids, MI: Zondervan, 1988), 174. See the responses by Charles C. Ryrie, *So Great Salvation* (Wheaton, IL: Victor, 1989), and Zane C. Hodges, *Absolutely Free!* (Grand Rapids, MI: Zondervan, 1989).

12. MacArthur, *The Gospel According to Jesus*, 176.

13. A. W. Tozer, *I Call It Heresy!* (Rockville, MD: Wildside Press, 2010) 7, 13.

14. See Luke 8:43–44, 9:11–17; John 8:3–11, 11:1–25.

15. Genesis 7:7, 22:8; Exodus 3:2, 13:22; Numbers 16:32; Ezekiel 10:10; Daniel 3:25.

16. Genesis 3:13–15; Joshua 6:17; Daniel 4.

17. Horatius Bonar, "Not Faith but Christ," www.the-highway.com/Faith_Bonar.html.

18. Dietrich Bonhoeffer, *The Cost of Discipleship* (New York: MacMillan, 1959), 43–45.

19. *Cambridge Greek Testament for Schools and Colleges*, "Commentary on Philippians 3:1" (1896), www.studylight.org/com/cgt/view.cgi?bk=php&ch=3. Public domain.

20. This case is ably made by Samuel C. Smith in "A Critique of *Bonhoeffer Speaks Today: Following Jesus at All Costs*," in *Journal of the Grace Evangelical Society*, Autumn 2007, www.faithalone.org/journal/2007ii/smith%20bonhoeffer.pdf.

21. Bonhoeffer, *The Cost of Discipleship*, 45. Emphasis in the original.

22. I. D. E. Thomas, comp., *A Puritan Golden Treasury* (Carlisle, PA: Banner of Truth, 2000), 166.

23. J. Israelstam, quoted in "A Fence around the Torah," Elijahnet, www.elijahnet.net/A%20FENCE%20AROUND %20THE%20TORAH.html.

24. Madeleine L'Engle, *A Wrinkle in Time* (New York: Farrar, Straus and Giroux, 1962).

25. Barna Group, "What Americans Believe about Universalism and Pluralism," April 18, 2011, retrieved March 26, 2014, https://www.barna.org/barna-update/faith-spirituality/484-what-americans-believe-about-universalism-and-pluralism#. UzLmtyjIboA. For example, an increasing number of younger Christians accept the premise that "Christians and Muslims worship the same God."

26. From the hymn "There's a Wideness in God's Mercy," by Frederick W. Faber, 1854.

27. C. S. Lewis, *The Weight of Glory* (New York: Touchstone, 1996), 29.

28. H. Richard Niebuhr, *Christ and Culture* (New York: Harper and Row, 1951), 45ff.

29. Niebuhr, *Christ and Culture*, 190ff.

30. Walter Rauschenbusch, *Christianity and the Social Crisis* (New York: Macmillan, 1910), 65.

31. Conversation between the author and a career missionary now working in a Muslim country. Name withheld for security reasons. If anyone has credibility in the social dimensions of the gospel, it is my friend, who lives and works in an emerging nation, training surgeons. He offers to pray with every one of the tens of thousands of patients he treats, and offers to share the gospel.

32. Adapted from a tweet by @jdgreear, November 20, 2009, https://twitter.com/jdgreear/status/5897343047.

33. Thayer and Smith's *The NAS New Testament Greek Lexicon*, 1999, www.biblestudytools.com/lexicons/greek/nas/kosmos.html.

34. Lewis Sperry Chafer, *Systematic Theology*, vol. 2, *Angelology-Anthropology-Hamartiology* (Dallas, TX: Dallas Seminary Press, 1947), 99–102.

35. Malcolm Gladwell, *Blink: The Power of Thinking without Thinking* (New York: Little, Brown, 2005), 3ff.

36. Gladwell, *Blink*, 5.

37. Gladwell, *Blink*, 8.

38. Dorothy Sayers, *Letters to a Diminished Church* (Nashville, TN: W Publishing, 2004), 49.

39. Lewis Sperry Chafer, *Grace: The Glorious Theme* (Grand Rapids, MI: Zondervan, 1950), 3.

40. Mark Noll, *The Scandal of the Evangelical Mind* (Grand Rapids, MI: Eerdmans, 1994), 3.

41. See various studies nicely summarized by Collin Hansen in "Why Johnny Can't Read the Bible," *Christianity Today* online, May 24, 2010, www.christianitytoday.com/ct/2010/may/25.38.html.

42. David Kinnaman, quoted by Audrey Barrick, "Study: Few Americans Embrace Traditional View of God," in *Christian Post*, www.christianpost.com/news/study-fewer-americans-embrace-traditional-view-of-god-27546.

43. Sayers, *Letters*, 49.

44. Sayers, *Letters*, 49.

45. *Wikipedia*, s.v. "Stampede," http://en.wikipedia.org/wiki/Stampede.

46. Michael Green, *Evangelism in the Early Church* (Grand Rapids, MI: Eerdmans, 1985).

47. Green, *Evangelism*, 238.

48. Green, *Evangelism*, 238.

49. Green, *Evangelism*, 239.

50. Green, *Evangelism*, 246.

51. Green, *Evangelism*, 245.

52. Green, *Evangelism*, 249.

53. From the poem by C. T. Studd, pioneer missionary, http://hockleys.org/2009/05/quote-only-one-life-twill-soon-be-past-poem. Public domain.

54. D. Martyn Lloyd-Jones, *Preachers and Preaching* (Grand Rapids, MI: Zondervan, 1972), 140.

55. Frederick Zugibe, *The Crucifixion of Jesus* (New York: M. Evans, 2005), 22. Zugibe was a forensic pathologist and medical examiner.

56. Zugibe, *Crucifixion of Jesus*, 36–37.

57. *Wikipedia*, s.v. "Crucifixion," https://en.wikipedia.org/wiki/Crucify.

58. For details, see *Wikipedia*, s.v. "Jehohanan," https://en.wikipedia.org/wiki/Jehohanan.

59. Zugibe, *Crucifixion of Jesus*, 100.

60. For the discussion, see Zugibe, *Crucifixion of Jesus*, ch. 7, 103–22.

61. D. A. Carson, *The Gospel According to John*, The Pillar New Testament Commentary (Grand Rapids, MI: Eerdmans, 1991).

62. Gerald L. Borchert, *The New American Commentary: An Exegetical and Theological Exposition of Holy Scripture*, John 12–21, vol. 25B (Nashville, TN: Broadman & Holman, 2002), 272–73.

63. Leon Morris, *The Apostolic Preaching of the Cross*, 3rd ed. (London: Tyndale Press, 1965). See Morris's table of contents for the list of topics.

64. Morris, *Apostolic Preaching*, 143.

65. Morris, *Apostolic Preaching*, 250.

66. George Bennard, "The Old Rugged Cross," 1913.

67. S.W. Gandy, quoted in Carson, *The Gospel According to John*, note on John 19:30.

68. "Simpson Devotional: Inspirational Readings by A.B.Simpson," www.cmalliance.org/devotions/simpson?mmdd=0428.

69. Oswald Chambers, *My Utmost for His Highest* (New York: Dodd, Mead, 1935), July 23.

70. Lewis Sperry Chafer, *Systematic Theology*, vol. 3 (Dallas, TX: Dallas Seminary Press, 1948), 325.

71. Adapted from Donald Grey Barnhouse, *Expositions of Bible Doctrines Taking the Epistle to the Romans as a Point of Departure* (Grand Rapids, MI: Eerdmans, 1966).

72. S. Lewis Johnson, "Once Saved, Always Saved; or, The Doctrine of the Perseverance of the Saints—1," www.sljinstitute.net/sermons/doctrine/pages/saints1.html.

73. Louis Berkhof, quoted in Johnson, "Once Saved."

74. John Rippon, "How Firm a Foundation," 1787.

75. Quoted in S. Lewis Johnson, "Assurance," http://sljinstitute.net/basic-bible-doctrine/assurance/.

76. John Murray, *Redemption Accomplished and Applied* (Grand Rapids, MI: Eerdmans, 1955), 155.

77. Augustine, quoted in Bishop Jewell, *Defense of the Apology* (1570).

Bill Giovannetti is the senior pastor of Northern California's Neighborhood Church. He teaches at A.W. Tozer Theological Seminary and is a fresh voice within today's grace movement. Bill merges theological insight with humor and a pastoral heart. He has inspired thousands to shed legalism and embrace God's grace in Christ.

Connect with Bill at:
BillGiovannetti.com
Twitter.com/BillGiovannetti
Facebook.com/Bill.Giovannetti